The Anti-Racist Media
Manifesto

T0273753

The Manifesto Series

David Buckingham, *The Media Education Manifesto*

Natalie Fenton, Des Freedman, Justin Schlosberg and Lina Dencik, *The Media Manifesto*

Anamik Saha, Francesca Sobande and Gavan Titley, *The Anti-Racist Media Manifesto*

Silvio Waisbord, *The Communication Manifesto*

Barbie Zelizer, Pablo J. Boczkowski and C. W. Anderson, *The Journalism Manifesto*

Anamik Saha
Francesca Sobande
Gavan Titley

————

The Anti-Racist
Media Manifesto

polity

First published in 2024 by Polity Press

Polity Press
65 Bridge Street
Cambridge CB2 1UR, UK

Polity Press
111 River Street
Hoboken, NJ 07030, USA

ISBN-13: 978-1-5095-5983-1
ISBN-13: 978-1-5095-5984-8(pb)

A catalogue record for this book is available from the British Library.

Library of Congress Control Number: 2024935709

Typeset in 11 on 15pt Sabon by
Cheshire Typesetting Ltd, Cuddington, Cheshire
Printed and bound in Great Britain by CPI Group (UK) Ltd, Croydon

For further information on Polity, visit our website:
politybooks.com

Contents

1

Why an Anti-Racist Media Manifesto?

Stick 'racism' into a Google news search sometime, and we wager that you'll come across headlines every bit as predictable as a soap opera storyline. Racism is sometimes revealed, often alleged and always denied. In headlines, it is often suspended in inverted commas as an unproven 'accusation', a convention that casts suspicion on both accused and accuser, and protects media sources from being seen as *too political*.

Racism is everywhere in our media, but it is, at the same time, curiously marginal. Pumped out and up in headlines, it is prime-time content. But go looking for sustained and considered engagement, and all too often the news search comes up short. It is just out there in the world, and when it is expressed through – often shocking – human actions, the media merely report it.

However, racism is not a static condition. It is reproduced, cultivated and mobilised by institutions and structures, and by social and political actors working through them. Media do not merely reflect events, hold a mirror to reality or tell things as they are. They mediate and shape. They intervene in social and political realities; they are actors, too.

Knit these basic observations together, and we arrive at a dynamic that anti-racist activists have long struggled with, and against. Media do not just reflect a racist world, they are often active in perpetuating and extending it. The ways in which this happens are often more complex than crude, but this does little to diminish their significance. Of course, media also do much to unmask and challenge racism. That the ways in which they do so are often more piecemeal than sustained does not fully diminish their significance either.

But, for all that, right now, it is time for something more.

The current moment is contradictory. It is characterised by the renewed anti-racist and anti-colonial commitment of social movements, and a more diffuse if still important anti-racist sentiment in public culture. It is also marked by the open and often gleeful resurgence of racist politics and discourse, driven by far-right forces and all too often indulged and mimicked across what was once regarded as the 'conventional' political spectrum. This antagonism is taking place, and also given shape, by the deep and frequently unpredictable penetration of media networks and market logics into social and political life. In this environment, racism circulates as content, is exchanged as commodity, and enjoyed as the stuff of spectacle.

It is in this context that we require an actively anti-racist media, and that is the subject of this manifesto.

* * *

Until relatively recently, it has been possible for liberal democracies in the 'West' to reproduce a dominant sense of themselves as *post-racial*. This is the conviction that racism has been overcome, rather than a straightforward denial of racism's existence. It is a powerful sense that racism has largely been consigned to the past, and that what remains is marginal and episodic, little more than the preserve of extremist acts and ignorant ideas.

The global surge in Black Lives Matter (BLM) protests in 2020 shattered these myths, which in truth had been fragile for some time. The preceding years demonstrated that such myths could not survive the intensification of a spectacular, racialised

3

politics, be it Trumpism and the fomenting of ethnonationalism in the US, or the full-throated 'populist' surge in many European nations.

Nor could they endure the evidence of the implacable realities of structural and imperial racism. The brutal calculus of the 'Windrush scandal' in the UK. The Islamophobic security and coercive 'integration' apparatus brought to bear over decades on Muslims. The heightened vulnerability of Black, Brown and Asian communities to Covid-19. The quotidian brutality and spectacular slaughter meted out by the Israeli state on Palestinian people. These matters have challenged the dominant complacency regarding racism's presumed marginality in political calculation, social relations and cultural life.

It is in this context that the BLM and anti-racist protests of 2020 precipitated a moment of so-called 'racial reckoning' across national settings and within institutions, structures, organisations and interpersonal relations. Particularly when informed by Black feminism and feminisms of the Global South – which address the interlocking nature of oppressions and the harmful impacts of geo-cultural power relations – this sustained mobilisation was profoundly intersectional, underlining how the interplay of racism with misogyny and class violence

4

impacts on people's access to rights and a liveable life.

One notable outcome of this period of contestation is the widespread attention that has been given to the key roles and responsibilities of media, and the ambivalence of media representation for anti-racist goals. Through reporting and commentary in this period, media played an integral role in raising awareness around specific injustices and bringing attention to BLM and other anti-racist movements. Some mainstream coverage also delegitimised the movement by following the normal routines of framing protest, particularly Black protest, as a threat to public order (Reid & Craig 2021).

Social media, for all their manifest problems, have helped publics to 'talk back' to media representations, journalistic frameworks and state rhetoric. During the BLM protests, they were important not only in disseminating important video footage and visual evidence, but in forging relations between activists and journalists that broadened the source base for coverage. Concomitantly, the same platforms enabled state surveillance of anti-racist organisers and dissenting actions. Social media, obviously enough, cannot be regarded as straightforwardly useful to anti-racism.

The tumultuous transformation of Twitter into X, since its 2022 purchase by Elon Musk, is one of many examples of social media's instability and the perilous potential for such platforms to shift in ways that produce real risks rather than contingent goods. The discourse churn of social media has provided a substantively unregulated environment for a dense ecology of far-right media to take shape. Despite liberal fears of 'echo chambers' leading citizens into 'polarisation', these emergent formations have steadily been integrated into the hybrid media system, pushing the 'balance' of many national media systems even further to the right. These ongoing contradictions provide important opportunities for reflection and intervention.

The manifesto engages with the question and problem of racism and media at a particular historical moment which is characterised by: the not-quite-aftermath of BLM and the Covid-19 pandemic; an inflation crisis which primarily punishes working-class people; the instability, nationalism and militarisation prompted and legitimised by Russia's disastrous invasion of Ukraine; the intensifying settler colonialism and genocidal violence of Israel in Palestine; and the continued, shape-shifting insurgence of ultra-nationalist and racist political movements.

Why an Anti-Racist Media Manifesto?

At least part of this acute, contemporary reactionary desire is a backlash against anti-racist and other social and political movements (at the time of writing, Palestinian solidarity movements seeking a ceasefire in Gaza were being vilified across Europe merely for existing and were denounced by the UK's then-Home Secretary as 'hate marches'). The rebranding of Twitter as X was presented as a way, according to its new owner, of combating the 'mind virus' of 'wokeness', in practice resulting in significant increases in hate speech, racial insults and extremist content and accounts (Frenkel & Conger 2022). Moreover, it is a politics increasingly articulated through an assault on the perceived gains not only of anti-racism, but of feminism, queer politics, ecological movements and activism for trans rights. Our adversaries are nothing if not intersectional.

In this ambivalent context, this manifesto makes an urgent effort not simply to make media 'less racist'. Instead, we must ask how media systems, policies and practices can be transformed in ways that actively challenge the production of racisms. Our focus here is not the plethora of community, radical and independent media that have already embraced this task. Nor, at the other end of the spectrum, is it the lucrative networks of commercial media that circulate racism as content and commodity, a spectacular invitation to reactionary pleasure. Instead, we are predominantly concerned with the centre that does not hold: the newspapers historically oriented to a democratic liberalism that abhors racism but 'does not see race'; the public service broadcasters who embrace diversity but never fully adjust their guiding idea of who the public really is; the digital media outlets who demand that staff have their own online presence but do nothing to protect them from online harms; social media platforms with robust community guidelines but who seem reluctant to actually confront racist abuse.

How could and should such media address the interconnected nature of racism and other forms of structural oppression? What could and should a truly anti-racist media look and act like? Addressing these questions is the purpose of the *Anti-Racist Media Manifesto*.

Racism and anti-racism now

Racism, as Ambalavaner Sivanandan famously put it, 'does not stand still' (1990). Contrary to the post-racial attempt to remove it from history and render it as nothing more than a moral issue,

Sivanandan emphasises its historical character, and how particular populations are *racialised* through specific socio-economic relations under capitalism, political practices and ideologies in the nation state. However, racism does not stand still also in the sense that it is opposed, and Sivanandan's analysis thus encourages us to be attentive to how political struggles transform racism's articulation.

Precisely because it does not stand still, racism is notoriously difficult to define. In a media economy characterised by 'hot take' simplifications, gloating pundits regularly turn this complexity against anti-racists, accusing them of 'making everything about race'. In so doing, they attempt to restrict public understandings of racism to overt forms of prejudice or extremism, a restriction which reflects the media industry's preoccupation with spectacle. Beyond this deliberately cultivated confusion, it is also the case that talking about structural factors can seem, paradoxically, too intangible. Institutional racism, for example, is a term that has entered popular vernacular in relation to hegemonically white institutions such as the police force, and to a lesser extent media. Yet its treatment often slips into an approach that is focused on removing a few 'bad apples' rather than addressing the systemic racist practices upon which those institutions are built.

This is the broader, deeper problem recognised by this manifesto. Racism is a structural and political form of oppression. But what does that mean, in practice, in our societies today? In a 2021 essay on Covid-19 and 'systemic racism', Gary Younge considers the intersection of BLM-inspired protests in Britain with the clearly racialised consequences of the pandemic, manifested by significant disparities in mortality in Britain between Black and Asian, and white groups. 'The virus does not discriminate on grounds of race', Younge notes, 'it didn't need to. Society had done that already.'

What Younge demonstrates is that racism is part of the broader social system, and its effects can be clearly seen. Higher levels of precarious employment meant that 'ethnic minorities' were more likely to have to continue contact work – such as in 'key' and 'essential' retail and healthcare roles – and overcrowded housing in marginalised urban areas made self-isolation more difficult. While acknowledging the phenomenon of racism directed at East Asian people during the pandemic, Younge dissects how Covid produced the form of racism that dominant post-racial sensibilities recognise and condemn, and the forms of racism that they allow to hide in plain sight:

at the very moment when the nation's consciousness was raised to the issue of racism through Black Lives Matter, we were presented with a clear example of how racism operates through Covid. Notwithstanding the handful of cases where non-white people were spat at, sometimes while being showered with racial epithets, there is no suggestion that anyone tried to deliberately make them ill with Covid. In other words, they were not disproportionately affected because individual people with bad attitudes did bad things to them. Their propensity to succumb to the virus wasn't primarily the result of people's uncouth behaviour, bad manners, crude epithets or poor education. For while all of those things are present, it is the systemic nature of racism that gives it its power and endurance.

It is this systemic nature that animated the global resurgence of activism driven by BLM and movements acting in solidarity in 2020 and beyond. When protests erupted across the United States on 26 May against the police murder of George Floyd, the collective emotion expressed was deeply personal but also political – grief and anger elicited by the intensively mediatised sadism he was subjected to. Justice for George Floyd may have been what sparked the protests, but these demands for justice transcended his individual treatment to encompass the established history of police violence against African Americans and ethnic minorities, and the equally implacable track record of impunity for these killings. This history of violence, in turn, was protested as a manifestation of 'systemic racism' in the United States, that is, an unequal exposure to lethal violence that is one of the many forms of discrimination and inequality experienced by Black and other racialised people in the US.

As vigils and protests spread beyond the United States, they became not only important acts of solidarity, but of translation. They drew links between racism in the US and racism in other national contexts – they contended that if we look here, and not just over there, there is racism. It is not exactly the same there as here, but we can make important connections. Activists in France defied a ban on solidarity marches to commemorate not only George Floyd but Adama Traoré, a young Black man murdered by police in 2016. The lack of accountability for his death was also linked to structural racism in France, but one produced by a different history of colonialism and post-imperial migration, and experienced differently in a state that officially 'refuses to see race' (this refusal has endured the 2023 police murder of Nahel Merzouk in Nanterre, which led to widespread urban revolt against state racism).

Elsewhere, activists connected racist systems to the lethal inequalities produced by the borders of nation states, and those of the European Union. Protests in Greece, for example, marked both the hypervisible murder of Floyd and the often invisibilised deaths at sea and in refugee camps enforced by Fortress Europe. In the contexts we write from, similar mobilisations occurred. Refugee-led movements in Ireland intensified their contestation of the state system of 'direct provision' that sequesters asylum seekers in limbo for years. In England and Wales, community groups protested police strip-searches of Black children, who are eleven times more likely to be treated that way than their white peers. In Scotland, people worked tirelessly to bring attention to the ongoing inquiry into the death of Sheku Bayoh, a Black man who died after being 'restrained' by police in 2015.

Transnationally, 2020 instigated a period of collective mobilisation to address racism and other interconnected oppressions, and this manifesto has taken inspiration from its courage and insistence. Yet it is also motivated by disquiet as to the force of the 'backlash' which has intensified in its aftermath, one which has animated multiple forms of racism in a context of both geopolitical instability and democratic flux. Critical to these reactionary currents is a concerted assault on forms of anti-racism, from sensational fabrications as to the influence of 'critical race theory' in the US, to the endless, gleeful production of 'wokeness' in the UK, to mendacious political attacks on the problem of 'decolonial thinking' and 'Islamo-leftism' in France. The flourishing of determined opposition to racism – as well as attempts to understand it and contest it through a reckoning with coloniality and nationalism – has been met by the bellicose assertion *that anti-racism has gone too far.*

This is not a novelty of so-called 'cancel culture' or the 'war on woke'; far from it. In a syndicated column published in 1965, William Buckley Jr, founder of the conservative journal *The National Review*, asked his readers the question, 'Are You Racist?', in which he argued that the word 'racist' was being used 'indiscriminately', its meaning diluted by making everything into a question of racism, preventing both a focus on 'real racism' – that is, Hitler – and leading to innocent people being denounced for simply trying to tell the truth as they see it (see Buccola 2019: 327–328). That is, three years before the assassination of Martin Luther King Jr, anti-racism had *already gone too far.*

Why an Anti-Racist Media Manifesto?

What is new is the extent to which political actors on the convergent right-to-far-right spectrum have been prepared to frame anti-racism as having now gone so far *that it constitutes an anti-democratic threat*. It shuts down freedom of speech, 'politicises' everything, and undermines the nation and 'shared values' by insisting on the problem of structural racism. Up is down, and so in this context European governments have concluded that it is the democratic thing to do to restrict protests and physically police protesters, intensify surveillance of student politics and activist groups, intervene in academic freedom, and defund and proscribe organisations, all the while proclaiming their opposition to racism and violence. In the context of this authoritarian turn, we need meaningful public commitments to anti-racism, and the media are critical to this.

Racism and media, now

Efforts to build towards this must recognise that the 'racial reckoning' was a profoundly ambivalent period for mainstream media outlets. The spectacular event-focused coverage of the moment, in Gary Younge's assessment, left the notion of systemic racism 'unreported, misreported or unexplained' and thus for much of the public, debates about it resembled 'walking into a movie halfway through to witness a car chase and struggling to work out who is pursuing whom and why'. Recent research on the coverage of BLM in UK newspapers details positive change as time went on, though while mentions of structural racism and its significance increased, analysis did not necessarily follow suit, and a focus on 'bad actors' and mainstream exemption endured (Bremner 2023). In the US, independent media and the 'Black press' deepened their commitment to reckoning with racism's prevalence in US society, and journalists of colour in mainstream media led a revolt against practices that restricted their reporting to 'bothsides-ing' opinions on the existence of racism, and that positioned them as 'too invested' and thus lacking in – an always mythic – objectivity.

The issues amplified in this period, of course, have been known for a very long time. News norms and values have long been critiqued for the ways in which they deem stories, and those who people them, as worthy of coverage, or not. On the terrain of representation, the casual distortions of stereotyping and the ambivalences of framing have for decades prompted opposition to how media reproduce and circulate racialised images and assumptions. Black feminist work points out the effects of interconnected anti-Black racism, misogyny and sexism – known as *misogynoir* (Bailey & Trudy 2018; Bailey 2021). Just as misogynoir results in the grassroots work of Black women and non-binary people rarely being affirmed amid mainstream framings of anti-racism, it also impacts who is (and is not) likely to benefit from media diversity initiatives.

In sum, minoritised people in the news and broader forms of media have tended to be invisible, or hypervisible, or objectifying combinations of both, whether it is the over-representation of Black people in relation to news stories on crime and social disorder, the invisibility of the most marginalised in society such as Traveller/Gypsy communities, or the spectacular appearance of populations subject to imperialism and colonialism when extreme violence or sociopolitical chaos forces its way into the hierarchies of 'newsworthiness'.

These representational patterns have, of course, been supplemented by a relatively new trend in the world of entertainment where Black, Brown and Asian people are now a ubiquitous presence. While the superdiversity we encounter on our screens (and in our ears) appears progressive, inside the media industries it is business as usual, as the status quo learns to capitalise, albeit clumsily at times, on global audiences' demands for more diverse content, including through 'their own voices' (that is, stories told by the marginalised who historically have been mainly (mis)spoken for).

As almost anybody with a social media account will know, racism festers in the digital space. The dynamics between racism and online media play out in many ways, including in the form of racist memes and other types of digital content that, by decontextualising and recontextualising popular culture symbols, reframe them to push far-right propaganda. Scholars and activists have drawn attention to how the supposedly neutral and objective data-driven algorithms and recommendation systems that shape our consumption of media are in fact 'hardwired' with racial biases (Noble 2018) that marginalise the content of Black, Brown and Asian activists and creators, while amplifying the content of far- and alt-right 'celebrities'.

Thus, criticism of how media and communications play a systemic role in the reproduction of racism must now encompass a considerable range of infrastructures, policies and practices. Given this, what does it mean to seek an anti-racist media future?

Anti-racism and media, now

Anti-racism is mutable because it demands far more than simply opposition to racism. And, as anti-racist movements combat a range of different forms of racism and do so on the basis of sometimes divergent understandings, politics and desires, the field of anti-racism is complex and sometimes fractious. Further, anti-racism has, after BLM, been taken up in distinctly contradictory ways. As Arun Kundnani has recently argued, while mainstream political discourse hummed with mentions of structural racism, this widespread acknowledgement of the problem did little to shift dominant modes of response away from individualising approaches. In fact, precisely the opposite, as 'everywhere you looked white liberals were talking about how to challenge unconscious biases, reduce micro-aggressions in interpersonal relationships, better represent diverse identities, educate away individual prejudices, and stop right-wing extremism' (2023).

Relatedly, there is the emergence of what sociologist Jo Littler (2017) calls a 'popular' form of anti-racism engaging with racial inequalities on the terms of 'diversity'. With particular pertinence for our manifesto, what is distinct about this mode of anti-racism is its keen interest in media as a site of racial injustice. Yet the turn to diversity to explain and address racial inequality in society is as limited as the *superdiversity* of contemporary media trends, characterised by reductive expressions of the politics of representation, be it counting faces or ticking boxes. This form of 'popular' anti-racism is easily incorporated and leveraged to corporate advantage; witness the statements released by nearly all the major media corporations in support of the 2020 Black Lives Matter protests, which was more likely to result in an increase in brand value rather than improve the working lives of the few Black workers inside the organisation.

In short, increased discussion of anti-racism in society or the media does not necessarily help build a more anti-racist world. Neither does too much loose talk of 'the media', for that matter, nor idealistic and thus abstract treatments of what 'it' should do. Such airy prescription is not the purpose of a manifesto. Instead it must work from understanding why we are in the situation we are in, and what we can make possible through its contradictions, dynamics and tensions.

The manifesto enters the debate at a moment of increased discussion *within* media *about* media and its complicity in racism. What it seeks to speak to is an urgent need, expressed by media professionals, activists and the general public, to better understand the different ways in which forms of media are active forces in the production of racisms and interlocking forms of structural oppression, while also providing resources and possibilities for resisting racialised politics and logics (which are also always gendered and classed, as well as being impacted by geopolitical histories and power relations). Media is a space where racisms are reproduced, but also a terrain where they can be resisted and challenged. In this ambivalent context, this short intervention identifies three key areas of the reproduction of racism in the media, and considers what can change, and how.

Firstly, we address issues of balance, objectivity and impartiality, forms of professional media detachment which seek to place mainstream journalism and current affairs media outside of politics, ideology and societal structures. As a consequence, not only do such practices and assumptions reproduce exceptional accounts of racism's meaning, obscuring any capacity to represent the consequences of structural racism. They also obscure how mainstream current affairs media reproduce racism through these practices and editorial assumptions. That is, by refusing to 'see' structure, they ensure that media work structurally. Long contested by radical journalism, these practices and assumptions have been the subject of significant dissent since 2020, as journalists with minority backgrounds in particular have contested the requirement to treat 'racism' not as a dimension of society and politics but as a subject of circuitous debate and potential controversy, perpetually suspended in quotation marks.

At the same time, the resurgence of the far right has led to ongoing conflict about how practices of 'balance' result in their platforming or mainstreaming. This established dilemma is now heightened by the political complexity of the modern far right, and by their media expertise, versed in benefiting from the dynamics of 'balanced' debate. In this context, the challenge is not just one of developing anti-racist practices within institutions, but of active commitments to be countervailing in a media system where racism is both a commodity and a standing political resource in conflicted polities.

Secondly, we turn to popular culture, and the ascendency of diversity – as a discourse and as a set of practices – which shapes so much of the media we consume today. Diversity is the primary way that both mainstream media and popular anti-racism address issues of racial inequality. In this liberal mode, the representation and visibility of Black,

Why an Anti-Racist Media Manifesto?

Brown and Asian people, both in media content and inside media industries, is seen as an important social justice issue. While this has resulted in an explosion of racial difference on our screens, celebrating these depictions substitutes a thin politics of representation – and one that feeds the post-racial assumptions now under political pressure – for a sustained engagement with how the media industries continue to sideline and exclude.

Behind the camera, the plethora of diversity initiatives that have been enacted by media organisations to increase the representation of minoritised groups have had very little effect on the composition of the creative workforce, which remains overwhelmingly white. Diversity is being operationalised in ways that maintain the privilege of the status quo and prevent meaningful structural change. To move past this, we argue, anti-racist media must be very clear about its diversity politics. Diversification of existing institutions and agencies is necessary, but so is a focus on achieving a reformed political economy of media that will enable the aesthetic, cultural and political practices of minoritised cultural producers, and facilitate a transformative politics of representation.

Thirdly, we consider how the development of digital technology and online processes and dynamics impact on the reproduction of racism in digital media contexts, and shape the possibilities for anti-racism in these communicative spaces. Once again, we emphasise the 'duality' of digital media. Its platforms and networks provide the possibility to forge anti-racist solidarities, raise consciousness and build community, while simultaneously exposing people to multiple forms of harm and damaging forms of surveillance. This chapter considers the different affordances of social media for anti-racist activism, the relationship between structural inequalities and people's (in)access to internet technologies, the impact of artificial intelligence (AI) on (racialised) labour, the limitations of common 'digital rights' frameworks, and how pressures to self-brand online undermine digital anti-racist work. The thread running through these key themes is the power of Big Tech and the impossibility of transforming the reproduction of digital racism under these conditions of public dominance. If ever there was a moment to jettison the myth that digital networking has resulted in a transformative redistribution of power, it is now.

In the concluding chapter we build on these lines of critique to suggest avenues for change at different levels of media activity and organisation. We do so by focusing on practical proposals, crucial principles and an overall vision of an anti-racist media future.

Why an Anti-Racist Media Manifesto?

While the concluding chapter brings together key ideas from the preceding pages, it is also informed by prior and ongoing work by anti-racist organisers, other scholars and grassroots groups.

2

Out of Balance

The other crisis

As with other venerable and vulnerable liberal institutions, mainstream journalism largely *doesn't see race*. Even, or especially, when reproducing it. When made strange, and viewed from outside of journalism's rarefied, normative aspirations, this conceit is breathtaking. The world of nation states has been configured racially through colonialism, capitalism, nationalism and migration. The 'problem populations' marked out historically for extermination and exploitation continue, by and large, to be vulnerable to forms of state violence, socio-economic marginalisation and spectacular scapegoating, including through how they are represented in the media. In this view from everywhere, journalism's studied incapacity to treat racism systemically could be regarded as active misrecognition – surely, in a world forged in these ways, the watchdog thing to do is to assume that racism is present, until proven otherwise?

Instead, current affairs media has largely reproduced post-racialism's excitable constrictions. The individualised understanding of racism is not only dominant, but hypermediated. Spectacular coverage of racist incidents and utterances proliferates, inviting insta-punditry to adjudicate as to what is really racist, and what is not racist at all, the systemic circulation of media noise seeking the status of a fleeting morality play. As this content flows, ceaselessly and lucratively through channels of comment and reaction, what Arun Kundnani (2023) terms 'the racisms of our age' – 'routine sets of practices, bound up with global structures of power, often articulated in terms of liberal values' – grind on and grind down, largely outside the frame. This should be rendered strange, also. For the racialised citizens and denizens of often reluctantly multicultural states, this misrepresents the reality of societies in which they cannot hope to mirror this studied idealism and, well, simply *define* the racism of the border, the security apparatus, capitalist predation and nationalist animus out of their lives.

The reasons for this myopia are involved, certainly. A pronounced liberal and positivist orientation regards discourse on racism, beyond verifiable acts and utterances – preferably captured on smartphones – as straying into 'ideology', and thus 'activism'. It is also hard to see structures when the dominant field orientation places the institution of journalism outside of them. This 'exercise in unreflective quarantine from the world', our colleagues in the *Journalism Manifesto* (Zelizer et al. 2021) write, means that 'invoking widely used practices, oft-proclaimed values and publicly heralded standards has helped to produce and sustain a uniform and isolationist view of how journalism works'. These values and practices, of 'objectivity', balance and detached impartiality, seek to guarantee professional journalism's democratic role and claim to the truth. In practice they prevent it, or absolve it, from a full accounting of how collective democratic life is distorted by racialised structures and racialising politics. By reifying the erasure of race as professional neutrality, while orienting towards audiences resiliently imagined as white, they work to reproduce the political *whiteness* of professional journalism (which as an employment sector anyway remains predominantly white and middle class).

Much of the current discussion of mainstream journalism's inadequacy on race is conducted through criticism of these professional norms, norms which are more widely held to be 'in crisis' because of significant shifts in communications technology, political economy, informational politics and democratic legitimation. Indeed, current affairs media are produced in an industry and profession where narratives of crisis are now so widespread that they provide a curious form of stability. Increased corporate consolidation and the often oligarchic concentration of media power have increased professional precarity, which acutely impacts already marginalised social groups. The digital disruption of financial models, and assumed and expected audiences, exacerbates the tension between commercial imperatives and acting in the public interest. The algorithmic personalisation of news flows flattens source hierarchies and blurs the boundaries between news journalism and other genres of content.

There has been a marked erosion of journalistic status in a digital media ecology, allied to a longer-term multivalent decline in confidence in the press, also as an element of the wider crisis of expertise and institutional authority in hollowed-out, neo-liberal democracies. What Mark Andrejevic terms 'an era of informational overload' endlessly multiplies accounts of reality and drags journalism into the 'clutter blender', empowering a 'post-sceptical' politics that works to 'cast doubt on any narrative's attempt to claim dominance: all so-called experts are biased, any account partial, all conclusions the result of an arbitrary and premature closure of the debate' (2013). As a key element of this, social media platforms have driven a partial and ambivalent redistribution of public discourse. This has exposed journalism to important forms of critical scrutiny, and also to sustained reactionary attack aimed at eroding the very possibility of meaningful news (and the death-through-rebranding of Twitter has had consequences for the media work of minority background journalists, depriving them of a once-functional platform for broadcast and verification, and flooding their communicative space with hostile actors and content).

Journalism's racism problem – which rarely features in this kind of crisis checklist – is exacerbated by these developments, not caused by them. The problem of race in the news is historically established; what has changed is that this short period of 'racial reckoning' has irrevocably manifested it. Current affairs media's misrecognition and misrepresentation of racism as a structuring force has, as the post-racial cracks open, produced a crisis with at least three dimensions.

There is a *public* dimension. A 2023 Pew Research Center study of Black Americans' experiences with news found consistent patterns of disaffection with news coverage, regardless of age, gender or political affiliation (the study did not factor in socio-economic class). As well as concerns with negative and stereotypical portrayal, a majority of respondents criticised a tendency towards coverage that only 'covers certain segments of Black communities or is often missing important information'. Most strikingly, 'just 14% of Black Americans are highly confident that Black people will be covered fairly in their lifetimes'. This study stands in for the multiple ways in which traditionally marginalised, under-represented and stereotyped groups contest the default whiteness of imagined news audiences; demand a reconstruction of newsworthiness through a meaningful pluralism of issues, perspectives and experiences; and seek a renewed, ethical connection of journalism to a world where the abject generation of racisms is again a central feature of powerful political mobilisations.

There is, as this chapter examines, a clear *professional* dimension, as media workers of colour and from minoritised backgrounds more and more

31

openly confront journalism's evasiveness, refuse to amplify or normalise racist discourse, and insist on racial justice as a legitimate goal for media work. Finally, there is a *partisan* dimension. In media systems across the 'West', a renewed and confident far-right demands 'balanced' engagement with its racist discourse and politics from the public service media (PSM) and liberal titles they simultaneously undermine as decadent, elite luxuries. In many contexts, new forms of far-right-inclined platform media have combined with the established reactionary press to forge altered media ecologies that reproduce racism as both ideological commitment and business model. These media actors will never mention structural racism, other than to scoff at wokeness, but they know and enjoy their roles in it. This ongoing realignment shift raises questions for media suspended between democratic commitment and post-racial conviction. As racism circulates as clickable content and affective invitation, that is, as an increasingly systemic property, concerted anti-racist commitment is required.

Be objective

In a widely shared 2020 opinion piece, 'A Reckoning over Objectivity, Led by Black Journalists', Wesley Lowery points to the gap between journalism's aspirational values and the reality of newsrooms, where 'conversations about objectivity, rather than happening in a virtuous vacuum, habitually focus on predicting whether a given sentence, opening paragraph or entire article will appear objective to a theoretical reader, who is invariably assumed to be white'. Writing less than a month after the police murder of George Floyd in Minneapolis, Lowery honed in on objectivity as a key driver of professional journalism's lack of 'moral clarity' on racism in the United States.

As protestors occupied the streets and braved incessant police violence, Black journalists were 'publicly airing years of accumulated grievances, demanding an overdue reckoning for a profession whose mainstream repeatedly brushes off their concerns'. The lack of newsworthiness of 'Black and Brown neighbourhoods' unless seen through the lens of crime; the lack of even functional diversity in media organisations; euphemising racism to avoid accusations of bias; not taking seriously the differentiated threat of racism within actually existing publics; ignoring how abstract norms have served to further marginalise media workers of colour and from minoritised backgrounds as 'too close to the story'. Lowery's charge sheet, like so many compiled in this conjuncture of upheaval and opportunity, is lengthy but not close to complete.

While objective reporting elements are present in 'hard news paradigms' transnationally, the ideal of opinion-less, detached objectivity is primarily associated with journalism in the United States, and often celebrated in its origin story of modern professionalisation (Esser & Umbricht 2014). Despite this, it occupies a curious status in treatments of US journalism. Excised from the Society of Professional Journalists' Code of Ethics in the 1990s for its aspirational abstraction, it is often recentred in the same terms, as a noble, if perhaps unattainable, democratic ideal (Canella 2023). This symbolic attachment has been intensified by the much-vaunted 'crisis of trust' in mainstream media, where ideas of rebuilding trust through engaged and collaborative approaches collide with a conviction that doubling down on institutional neutrality and objective, factual provision is the only way to reconstruct lost authority.

For all this, there is little real consensus on what objectivity encompasses. Functionalist approaches describe it through lists of professional components. Sociological treatments emphasise its field-stabilising, ritual dimensions, where normative practices do not descend from abstract ideals but are shaped and contested over time. Carlos Alamo-Pastrana and William Hoynes's (2020) sharp summary of objectivity as norm and practice underlines how it

> affirms professional journalism as knowledge with an invisible standpoint ... [that] emphasises a two-sided version of balance, separating facts from opinion, attributing opinions to (preferably named) sources, an emphasis on description over interpretation, and an avoidance of highly charged language. These practices ensure that news is neither one-sided (by definition, since reporters include two sides) and contain expressions of opinion limited to the perspectives of news sources rather than journalists themselves. Following standard practices of objective reporting relieves journalists of the responsibility to account for the forces that structure their professional standpoint.

These elements are also easily reframed as a rap sheet. Let's take at least one illustrative charge, something mildly counter-intuitive, such as how the separation of facts from values often unwittingly serves the implacable dehumanisation of so much 'migration' politics. In their 1979 documentary for the Campaign against Racism in the Media, *It Ain't Half Racist Mum*, Stuart Hall and Maggie Steed[1] note acerbically that 'whenever programmes are made about Blacks the starting point is always numbers. And there's nothing factual television likes so much as a good number.' Exhibit A, a serious BBC current affairs programme investigating the question, 'How big is Britain's non-white population?', illustrating its growth through a graphic displaying how many 'Wembley stadiums of Black people' are now in the country. Numbers as facts, graphically objectified, not an opinion to be found, yet, 'If you always only talk about Blacks in relation to numbers, the audience cannot help but think that that must be the problem. The possibility that the problem might lie with white society is never considered.' That is, the force of structural racism is implicit in the journalistic frame, even as objective practice seeks to situate it outside of the society it is dispassionately reporting on.

Fast forward from the bad old days, to a BBC where such crude representations of multicultural Britain have long been institutionally unthinkable. Yet, this does not mean that the consequences of 'fact first' journalism have been systematically unthought. A 2019 study of BBC coverage of the

relatively recent category of 'climate refugees'
notes how it approaches it as a 'global scientific
phenomenon' (see Høeg and Tulloch 2019). What
this amounts to in practice is a default, dominant
sourcing of expertise from the Global North; a glar-
ing absence of refugee 'voices' (that is, the anyway
limited representational modality generically
accorded to refugees-as-victims); and a preoccupation with 'increasing but uncertain numbers' which,
in its speculative futurism, reproduces the exact
kind of numerical threat objectification crammed so
absurdly into Wembley Stadium. Here, again, forty
years on from the BBC's objective exercise in great
replacement thinking, the weight of racialisation,
through the anonymised and countable racial other,
presses on the frame.

It is, in (critical) theory, relatively established that
the conceit of objectivity not only misrecognises
race, but reproduces it. The positivist firewalling
of facts from values obscures and dehistoricises
processes of racialisation. The liberal insistence on
detachment suffuses the myth that journalism exists
outside of racist legacies, institutions and systems.
Nonetheless, what is notable about the BLM-
inspired media reckoning is the extent to which
it detonated within professional journalism itself.
Interventions such as Lowery's position objectivity

less as a fixed and coherent praxis than as a prism through which multiple failings and evasions can be refracted, and finally grasped. From the early summer of 2020, these entrenched problems were magnified from the very first in reporting on solidarity and justice protests across the United States.

Given the extent of police/state violence against protestors, an intense debate erupted around the need for photojournalists to protect the identities of protestors from further anti-Black brutality at the hands of the security apparatus. Images cannot but signify in a wider economy of meaning. More concretely, they are also routinely used as police evidence. Given this, an insistence on objectively capturing the moment (while bracketing all of the choices involved in photo composition and selection) and refusing to stray into 'activism' is to inescapably choose sides or have your side chosen for you. As William C. Anderson put it, 'After all, their subjects are people whose lives are enshrouded by racist subjugation. The reality is those who capture their likeness are acting as informants' (2020).

The established relationship of crime reporting to the police was also radically questioned. Objectivity's centring of 'official sources' in news writing has in practice meant that reports of what are gingerly termed 'police-involved shootings' heavily depend on police accounts. That these initial versions so often turn out to be patently untrue has, until recently, had vanishingly little impact on textbook objective practice.[2] Indeed, reporting on police killing of African Americans has often gone much further, colluding in the security forces' inevitable attempts at character assassination such as when *The New York Times* notoriously described the teenage Michael Brown, whose killing sparked mass protest in Ferguson, Missouri, as 'no angel'.

The most explosive crack in the edifice of objectivity ran through the resilient editorial assumption that media workers of colour and from minoritised backgrounds are 'too close to the story', or simply biased, when it comes to questions of racism. Objectivity, so white; requiring journalists to have no subjectivity or standpoint does nothing more than invisibilise the positions from which journalism is inevitably produced. Treating Black, Latinx or – the tiny cohort of – Indigenous reporters working outside of independent, Black and community media as too subjective to report what is happening in, or being done to, populations they identify or are associated with, enshrines whiteness as the neutral guarantor of objectivity. To be racialised is to be perpetually suspected of excessive subjectivity.

Under conditions of sociopolitical conflict, where news brands are falling back on 'facts-first journalism' as a trust claim and commercial strategy, nothing less than total self-exclusion from political reality will do. And not even then; in one newspaper an African American journalist was removed from coverage of the BLM protests for 'expressing an opinion' on Twitter held to compromise the objectivity of their reporting, and so was another reporter that didn't express any opinion at all.[3]

While this gatekeeping amounts to an essentialist diminishment of professionalism, it adds a deeper layer of condescension, that to oppose racism is automatically beyond the pale of journalism's stated democratic goals. This exclusion illuminates media complicity in racist structures at the point where it attempts to mark the greatest distance.

Be impartial

Donald Trump's late-night discourse cabaret on the presidential Twitter account clarified a key labour relation of the digital age. Trollish content gets lashed out with minimal input and maximal glee, a ritual that custodians of the public sphere must treat with deliberative seriousness, investing time and resources in parsing, fact-checking and reporting. This relation has a particular valence when the provocation is deliberately racist. When Trump tweeted in 2019 that four Democratic congresswomen of colour should 'go back and help fix the totally broken and crime infested places from which they came', it kicked off a set of second-order debates in journalism as to whether it was legitimate to describe this as racist, or 'racist'. When, less than a month later, a far-right extremist posted a 'manifesto' on 8chan condemning a 'Hispanic takeover' before murdering twenty-three people at a Walmart in El Paso, Texas, Latino journalists underlined the importance of considering the relationship between elite racist rhetoric and 'radicalised' racist violence (Olivares 2019). The point was not simply to issue a moral condemnation of Trump. Rather, it was a recognition that it is critical to name racism as a political phenomenon in order to clearly examine how it is reproduced. There is no direct causality between Trump's comments and mass murder by a white supremacist, a relation the debate about hate speech is so often reduced to. Rather, there are structuring connections between spectacular eliminationist violence and the everyday racism of political expediency and nationalist maintenance of imagined community.

At the same time, the fraying but tenacious allure of detachment seeks to fix inverted commas to every mention of racism. In reporting on Trump's comments, the BBC Breakfast host Dan Walker asked his co-host Naga Munchetty how she felt about them, to which she replied 'absolutely furious and I can imagine lots of people in this country will be feeling absolutely furious a man in that position thinks it's ok to skirt the lines by using language like that'. After a complaint from one viewer, the BBC Editorial Complaints Unit found that Munchetty had breached impartiality guidelines that do not allow journalists to give an opinion about 'the individual making the remarks or their motives for doing so'. The decision was greeted by a significant public backlash, including an open letter from 'people of colour that work in the media and broadcasting in the UK' and which pointed out that racism could hardly be treated as a valid opinion on which impartiality can be maintained, and to expect individuals who can be subjected to racism to treat such contentions as valid has 'devastating and maybe illegal consequences for our dignity and ability to work in a professional environment' (Hirsch et al. 2019).

What does it mean to be impartial? In public debate, the terms objectivity, impartiality and balance are often used interchangeably, yet they carry varying weight and meaning in different media systems. If objectivity, broadly speaking, seeks to remove the subjectivity of the journalist from the production of knowledge, impartiality removes it from the conduct of public debate. It demands that all sides of an argument are presented, and that ideas and opinions are treated, within legal parameters, with equal detachment. This is a particular policy and ethical prerogative for a public service broadcaster, charged, in ideal terms, with representing the diversity and unity of the nation to itself. Nevertheless, this stated commitment does not really explain why the BBC was prepared to discipline a high-profile journalist for mild criticism of something so obviously racist that at least some mainstream outlets had felt liberated to finally take the inverted commas off. The public service broadcaster has, after all, been compelled over decades to engage with how impartiality guidelines are implicated in, for example, shaping negative 'debates' on immigration. Moreover, the BBC, like other media outlets, has noted the dangers of impartiality with respect to issues such as climate change, where 'you do not need a denier to balance the debate' (Carrington 2018). What, then, makes coverage of resurgent racism so particularly fraught?

Post-racial hegemony fixes racism as a moral evil, but also narrowly fixes its meaning in ahistorical and apolitical ways. In this framework, as Alana Lentin (2019) has argued, 'calling something racist' is only legitimate if it is based on 'the predominance of individualist moralism; the reliance on an overly narrow, strictly biological and hierarchical account of racism; and the universalisation of racism as equally practiced by all groups independent of status and power'. This investment in a correct definition is not simply about shared understanding. It is a particular kind of demand made in societies dominantly imagined as anti-racist and white, and it is a *demand for substantive control of what racism means.* If we know exactly what racism means, we can be categorically certain that everything else that happens is 'not racism'. With closure achieved on the meaning of racism, everything else becomes a question of debate, and the impartial hosting of debate is a democratic duty. Once again, it is in the moment of democratic valorisation that structural racism becomes most keenly apparent. Impartiality is not just an impediment to taking an anti-racist stand on BBC Breakfast. More fundamentally, its mechanistic application recuses organisations from developing necessary institutional knowledge as to how contemporary racisms work, discursively and politically. In so doing, it ensures implication in their reproduction.

The discipline enacted on Munchetty, therefore, was not just institutional. Invited by a BBC representative to share her experience on-air, she was censured by the BBC off-air for speaking from that position. Absurd as it sounds, she was disciplined for not deracialising herself before speaking about her experience of racism. By referring to Trump's irresponsibility in using his position of power to circulate widely recognised racial tropes, she breached guidelines by 'giving an opinion about the individual' behind the comment. In other words, for treating racism as something that is politically reproduced and legitimated. It is the irreducibly *political nature of racism* that impartiality seeks to evade. Much better to just host the debate, and transfer the costs of editorial evasion elsewhere.

One consequence of editorial disavowal is that the meaning of racism becomes a ritual subject of sensation in the 'opinion economy'. It provokes a debate that can be hosted in relation to any incident or accusation that flows through media culture, hinging on speculation as to whether the event in question is categorically racist, or not. The journalist Micha Frazer-Carroll describes feeling jaded by broadcast race 'debates' that never address structural racism but start with a producer's call, 'Someone has said something racist? Do I want to come on the show?' What transpires is often a 'culture war' set-up or a predictable 'debate' where 'the odds are stacked against the person of colour being inserted into the conversation; it becomes about fighting your corner and "proving" that racism exists to a sceptical panel of people with no real understanding of what racism looks like' (2020).

On a larger scale, reneging on any responsibility to understand how contemporary racisms work ensures that media logics of newsworthiness seamlessly complement the political desire to fixate on racialised populations as a constant and outsized focus of political attention. Throughout the first decades of this century, mainstream media in North America and Europe colluded in the integration politics of the 'War on Terror' era that rendered the lives and presence of Muslim people a consistent focus of political scrutiny, and thus public debate. 'To be at the sharp end of a nationalist politics', as Sivamohan Valluvan observes, 'is to know yourself not only as an outsider but also as an outsider who is actively and incessantly spoken of' (2019). Detachment assures that these attachments endure.

Be balanced

The distorting effect of impartiality in the politics of racism is now most acutely felt in the ease with which many far-right parties, movements and political entrepreneurs have been able to 'mainstream' their agendas and reference points as normal political issues worthy of public consideration. This is in no small part a consequence of ideological convergence on the right between traditional conservative parties seeking renewal and post-fascist parties repositioning themselves electorally (Renton 2019). It also owes much to the vulnerability of broadcast media; in particular, to a key dimension of 'populist' myth-making. We can leave aside here the circuitous debates on the meaning of populism merely to observe that the consistent claim of radical right populists to speak for a silent majority hits a nerve for media institutions whose audiences are fragmented and publics uncertain. This is intensified for many public service broadcasters, who are under relentless political attack from the right for being too costly, too liberal and too 'out of touch' with ordinary concerns. Under these conditions, why take the risk that this new movement or taboo-breaking firebrand that everyone is talking about on social media, and who is anyway telling you that they only want to defend women's rights, or free speech or national values, doesn't actually speak for those 'left behind' audience segments that you've been losing for years?

The expectation here is not that mainstream media enact a blanket cordon sanitaire around the far right. Broadcast guidelines for political parties, statutory forms of balance during election and referendum periods, informing the public about political developments; these are but some of the reasons why forming such a block is practically very difficult. Nonetheless, it has to be underlined that in accepting the gambit of populist ventriloquism, media are platforming movements whose politics are based on scapegoating other constituencies *within their publics*. That is, the often uncritical platforming of the far right privileges the desires of an imagined (white) audience over the dignity of an actual, multicultural public whose ongoing alienation with current affairs coverage is a matter of fact. The default invocation of balance, in this equation, is only credible if the editorial work which goes into shaping the spectrum of legitimate opinion is obscured. It is patronising to publics to present 'balance' as merely a representation of what is given, rather than owning it as an interventionist construction of what should apparently be. For all the editorial complexity involved, a basic axiom can be applied: 'balancing in' far-right actors and discourse further 'balances out' the public sphere for those who are the unwilling subjects of nationalist fixation.

The problem for liberal democratic media is that acquiescence with the forces that relentlessly accuse them of bias does not buy peace. It can never prove to its gleeful antagonists that it is not elitist, woke or politically correct. Victimhood is the animating affect of nationalist mobilisation. Far-right and 'populist' political strategy therefore allots media a structural, ideological role independent of actual practices. This is particularly evident when it comes to the endless sensation of the 'racism debate'. The refusal to come to terms with how racism is reproduced is a gift to a reactionary politics primed to seize on every mention of racism as an unfair accusation silencing the already silent majority. As noted, this is not novel, and in fact none of the ways in which public media and the broadly liberal mainstream are goaded into amplifying the far right are particularly new. What is now different is the media–political nexus in which they are being mobilised.

Firstly, attacks on established media are not just rhetorical. The gallery of far-right parties in power in the Nordic countries, for example, have all made it their business to target public service broadcasting once in government. These attempts to diminish public media are occurring in a period when the media ecology is being altered by the convergence of the established conservative press with a wide variety of newer reactionary media. These platforms, up to and including those associated with the extreme right, are no longer content to merely play the role of 'movement' or even 'alternative media'. They seek space in the formal media landscape by directly challenging journalistic authority, positioning themselves as keeping check on the mainstream's lack of objectivity and balance. The contemporary far right, therefore, cannot be understood through movements and parties alone. What are often euphemised as 'hyperpartisan' media play an increasing role not only in the dissemination but also in the generation of racist panics and media events, and circulate far-right thought far beyond what are traditionally regarded as far-right political actors.

While there are significant differences in scale and political orientation between older and newer actors in this converging media space, it is also clear that they increasingly form networks of exchange and legitimation that seek to steer public discourse even further to the right. This altered media ecology integrates an increasingly 'radicalised' established right-wing press; new, well-funded platforms and agencies, a proliferation of well-connected think tanks and Astroturfed actors savvy in their communications, action-at-scale by far-right entrepreneurs through social media channels.

This process has been well observed in the United States, with Benkler et al.'s (2018) work mapping the emergence of a 'distinct and insulated media system' engaged in 'asymmetric polarisation', that is, an all-out assault on the legitimacy of liberal mainstream media. In France, the aggressive takeovers conducted by the Bolloré group have resulted in a media empire that openly platforms the far right and which has led to unprecedented strikes and actions by resisting journalists.

Press and cross-media ownership in the UK is already notably oligopolistic, and the last years have seen concerted efforts to replicate this in the broadcast spectrum, with the establishment of two avowedly right-wing channels, TalkTV and GB News. The next stage in this pattern may well involve deeper convergence on the right and far right, as the hedge fund millionaire Paul Marshall, who owns GB News and *Unherd*, seeks to buy *The Daily Telegraph* and *The Spectator* (with additional funding from Ken Griffin, a major donor to hard-right US Republicans such as Ron DeSantis [Davis 2024]).

Such a move represents a shift from political affinity – all these titles are very close to the Conservative Party, and both GB News and *The Telegraph* regularly provide platforms for the hard right of the party – to financial and possibly editorial integration. This established form of media power and control must also be understood in terms of how it enmeshes with the digital media ecology. A 2024 investigation of Marshall's anonymised Twitter account by Hope Not Hate revealed a history of liking and retweeting conspiratorial racist material about the likelihood of a civil war between 'native Europeans' and 'fake refugee invaders'. This material was derived from a familiar network of Trumpian YouTubers, 'independent' media and far-right activists; that is, the milieu whose key ideas and ideological motifs are substantively circulated and laundered through the increasingly radicalised mainstream titles, in the name of free speech.

Even as systemic balance gets knocked further out of kilter by these aggressive manoeuvres, these initiatives legitimate themselves as necessarily democratic correctives. GB News, whose founding mission is to protect free speech against 'cancel culture and wokeness', presents itself as a pluralist counterbalance to BBC bias (Barnett & Petley 2022). The French channel CNews presents itself as a *chaîne pluraliste* even as over 80% of its contributors are drawn from the conservative and far right (Menuge et al. 2023).

The question then becomes, what does balance mean in media systems that are becoming dangerously unbalanced, and where well-funded and expansive media networks circulate to significant publics the ideas, provocations and talking points of a politics dedicated to little more than ensuring that 'problem populations' remain the problem? We return to this in the book's final chapter.

3

The Limits of Diversity and Representation

The turn to diversity

Having once been invisible, people of colour now feel *ubiquitous* in media culture, whether a Hollywood blockbuster, a sofa ad, a TikTok feed, or even a period drama. Yet, despite the proliferation of Black, Brown and Asian people on our screens, how do we make sense of the scenes behind the cameras, where the cultural industries remain overwhelmingly white, and its working conditions hostile towards marginalised groups? To repeat one of the key principles behind this manifesto, media is the space where racisms are actively produced, but it is also the space where racisms are to be resisted and challenged, not least by the marginalised. Hence one of the manifesto's main aims – and the purpose of this chapter – is to formulate strategies that facilitate the creative practice of Black, Asian and other racialised people working inside media that can help shift hegemonic understandings of race in media/society through the *politics of representation*.

It should be noted that diversity outside the context of media is a hotly politicised topic. Equality/ equity and diversity initiatives (EDI) as enacted in public institutions like schools, universities and public office are under attack from increasingly authoritarian right-wing governments. This, however, feels very different to how diversity is being operationalised in media. Media is a key institution through which the dominant culture in society maintains its status and privilege as well as economic dominance, but this nonetheless sits in tension with a democratic belief in the public value of media. Media can generate huge profits, but there is also a recognition of its role in creating a sense of national community and social cohesion. Such values undergird PSM that still play a significant, if lessening, role in socially democratic nations. In advanced capitalist nations like the US, where PSM is much less considerable, it was up to the civil rights movement to illuminate media as a key arena to help foster equality. Diversity discourse is shaped by these histories. But in the current moment there is a heightened appeal for diversity, driven by the demands and desires of global audiences (albeit in a way that, as we discuss, protects the status of global elites). A combination of these different forces has made the issue of diversity in media of significant public concern (just see #oscarssowhite and the seemingly annual furore over the whiteness of television and film award nominee lists), generating popular news content, and in turn, a churn of commentary on social media.

Thus, there is an understanding inside and out, that media need to become more diverse. Indeed 'diversity' has become the very language through which media make sense of and attempt to address the racial inequalities that exist. Yet, despite this emphasis on diversity, the composition of the media workforce remains as monocultural as it ever was. Our reference to diversity as a 'discourse' is purposeful: diversity is a form of *power/knowledge* that helps sustain rather than dismantle racial hierarchies. As this chapter argues, the goal of a truly anti-racist media is not to merely fix the diversity problem as it exists in media, but to do away with the language of diversity altogether. In its place we propose initiatives to be implemented at the structural level that are less fixated on the textual nature of representation and more focused on physically opening the field of representation. The aim of this chapter is to highlight the limits of diversity and the conception of representation that underpins it, and to argue for structural change to facilitate and support marginalised people working in media and their creative practice. In order to make media more anti-racist, we need to reject and move beyond the diversity paradigm.

The problem with diversity

Despite the protestations of conservative commentators, the overwhelming consensus in both the industry and the general public is that media needs to do better when it comes to the diversity of the people who work in it and the content it produces. This is rationalised in terms of moral/ ethical values; modern creative and cultural industries' very sense of self is based on being seen as open, liberal and, more importantly, *not racist*. But an economic rationale is increasingly employed too: in a fully global media marketplace, reaching wider, more diverse audiences offers immense commercial potential, and in order to engage those audiences, media need a diverse creative workforce. Diversity is shaping all spheres of media-making including corporate (both Big Tech and legacy media), PSM and even independent media.

Diversity as an approach can cover a range of initiatives that target a range of different concerns related to equality. On a very basic level it is focused on increasing the number of people from historically marginalised groups within an organisation. As perhaps the most visible form of difference, diversity is often framed in terms of race and ethnicity, but it also relates to class, disability, gender and sexuality. The problem of diversity is seen as one of access, and as such diversity initiatives are focused on facilitating entry for marginalised groups. These include setting targets for recruitment (it should be noted that quotas remain illegal in most Western nations and affirmative action rolled back in nations where it has been historically implemented, such as the US), training programmes and work placements specifically designed for these groups, mentorship schemes, and statements on job adverts that encourage applications from individuals belonging to groups who are under-represented. Media companies have a plethora of independent research to refer to that tracks how well their sectors are doing in increasing diversity both in the workforce and in media content (some high-profile examples include USC Annenberg's Inclusion Initiative and the Centre for Scholars and Storytellers based out of UCLA). Occasionally, a company will run a private audit of diversity in their content (for instance, a publishing house counting the number of books on a front list that have been written by Black authors). However, formal diversity policies are mostly focused on recruitment, with an assumption that increasing the diversity of the workforce will *automatically* lead to better representation of those groups in media content itself, which will in turn help engage new audiences (again, *diversity is good for business*). From a mainstream or *popular* anti-racist perspective, the emphasis on diversity feels progressive. At the very least, within this diversity paradigm, there is a recognition that media industries have overlooked racially and ethnically minoritised groups and are now trying to address this. But what has been the impact of diversity upon ongoing racial inequalities in media?

In terms of media content, Black, Brown and Asian people are today presented with undeniably more professional opportunities, though it is important to note that the industry remains predominantly white and middle class. The catalogues of the major streaming services feel not just diverse but *super-diverse*; it is difficult to *not* encounter a person of colour in a contemporary production. Following the success of Shonda Rhimes' *Bridgerton*, even the historically whiter-than-white period drama now features Black and Brown people as its default setting. Another apparent positive is how the racialised appear to have been liberated from historically entrenched stereotypes. No longer the servant, victim or antagonist, the Racial Other is now the main protagonist, leading both ordinary and extraordinary lives and seemingly unharmed by racism. But to what extent does this depiction of a post-racial society not just obfuscate but help exacerbate racial inequalities and injustice in real life? Diversity on our screens presents what Jo Littler (2017) describes as the *myth* of meritocracy – an image of society as a level playing field where everyone can succeed if they work hard enough no matter their (racial) background. Littler's argument is that this is not just idealised but ideologically constructed for the benefit of the status quo. As shall be made clear, we absolutely reject an approach that evaluates media in terms of how accurately it reflects a fixed, external reality. Yet the contrast between the social worlds that are conjured through the logics of diversity, where racism has apparently been overcome, and the actual lived experience of the poorest racially and ethnically minoritised groups, compounded by the racist, anti-migrant rhetoric and policies spewed out by the government, feels more than just stark. Critical media scholar Kristen Warner (2017) puts it more succinctly when she describes the type of diversity that we find in so much contemporary film and television production as simply 'plastic representation'.

The limits of diversity become even more pronounced when we look inside media. Creative and cultural industries remain overwhelmingly white. Despite decades of diversity initiatives, the make-up of the creative workforce remains broadly consistent, in that its whiteness is entrenched. This is borne out by the data from the UK and US, which are supposedly the two most progressive nations on issues of diversity. In the UK, research on creative and cultural industries shows that white people make up 95% of the publishing industry and 91% of the film, television, video and radio sectors compared to 87% of the entire workforce at large (Brook et al. 2020: 60–61). When we consider that the vast majority of these industries are based in London, where white people constitute about half of the total workforce, the lack of diversity in media feels even more pronounced. (Interestingly, when British public service broadcaster Channel 4 announced it was moving its headquarters to Leeds, one of the objections to the move from its predominantly white, middle-class employees was that no longer being centred in multicultural London would have a detrimental effect on the diversity of its workforce. Not only was this disingenuous but it ignores how Leeds itself has a large Black and Asian population.) Moreover, diversity is lacking even more at senior/executive level (Brook et al. 2020). In the US we find similar patterns. For instance, the latest 2023 UCLA Hollywood Diversity Report, which has been tracking racial/ethnic and gender diversity in US film and television for over a decade, notes that since 2019, although there has been some incremental improvement in certain areas of employment for racially minoritised groups, there has overall been a reduced proportion represented in the media workforce (UCLA Entertainment and Media Research Initiative 2023).

In summary, we see an overabundance of diversity in media content, though this is mostly superficial, a veneer to look at, rather than something that is meaningfully explored, and a dearth of diversity in the creative workforce, despite the numerous initiatives and schemes that have attempted to address this. Is it the case, then, that we need to formulate better diversity instruments to improve the racial and ethnic composition of workers inside media, especially in the senior, gatekeeping roles? We argue the opposite: that the problem is diversity itself, as it is conceptualised and operationalised.

The problem with the diversity approach is how it places too much emphasis on representation as an end goal. Of course, representation matters. The very premise of this manifesto is that specific racialised groups are treated – and indeed, represented – by media in dehumanising ways that stress their absolute difference, and inherent inferiority, whether based on spurious claims about genetics or backward cultural practices. Postcolonial theorists highlight how contemporary representations of race originate from the earliest encounters within colonialism; the Other as savage, denigrated on the one hand and exoticised on the other. In this regard, the interventions of racialised people inside media have had a radical effect in transforming the regime of representation. Stuart Hall's famous coinage of 'the politics of representation' (1988) was inspired by a shift that he identified in how Black and Asian people are represented in 1980s British cinema, driven by Black and Asian screenwriters and filmmakers. Not only were they transgressing the binary oppositions within which the postcolonial subject was trapped, but their articulation of *new ethnicities* demanded a radical overhaul of the very critical terms within which this

63

art was to be interpreted and read. Put simply, the impact of the new ethnicities moment was how it offered a new mode of representational politics that went beyond simply reversing negative representations of race with positive ones. It exploded this binary altogether.

But in the present moment we have returned to thinking about representation in simplistic ways. Rather than develop a new critical language to understand the complexity of the politics of representation that Hall had hoped for, we have regressed to a version of media representation that is measured in terms of accuracy and visibility. Analysing the representation of race becomes a tick-box exercise to ensure that all ethnic and racial minorities are present and correct. Audiences get into heated debates on social media on whether a particular culture is depicted authentically, or whether the characterisation of, say, a Black and/or Muslim subject is sufficiently accurate. Troublingly, a mode of liberal anti-racism cannot help but slip into this discourse. Hall stressed how the politics of representation is contingent and defined entirely by context. Contemporary representational-talk, however, has left behind nuance, and would rather enter a game of *diversity bingo*, ticking off minoritised groups as they appear in media, and shaming those people involved when such a group is not included or has been misrepresented.

This conception of representation in terms of visibility also underpins diversity initiatives inside media that are focused on recruitment. In the context of corporate media especially, with its culture of key performance indicators, diversity is approached in terms of a numbers problem. Media sociologist Herman Gray (2016) critiques a certain type of diversity-framing that links representation to demography that typifies media's approach to the issue. This sees diversity in terms of achieving a measure of representational parity. In Britain, nearly all corporate media have set themselves diversity targets (to reiterate, enforceable quotas cannot be set in the UK due to equality laws) based roughly around attaining parity with national demographics. Under this approach, diversity is reduced to a statistical problem to be solved rather than a process of tackling forms of racial discrimination.

There are several problems with measuring representation in terms of attaining demographic parity. Firstly, in many nations, these targets are unenforceable and, as such, they struggle to be met. Since positive discrimination/affirmative action is illegal in these contexts, media rely on relatively soft forms of positive action initiatives (as outlined above) to attract applicants from under-represented communities. (Perhaps more critically, they will also rely on employers not acting in a discriminatory fashion, even with unconscious bias training – another form of soft action.) The fact is, until media organisations are allowed (let alone, show willing) to employ positive discrimination/affirmative action, then targets will never be met.

Secondly, the numerical/representational approach to diversity inevitably leads to a tick-box mentality. The focus is on getting people from under-represented groups through the door. But once inside an organisation, there is less emphasis on supporting these people from marginalised backgrounds. Research shows that retention remains a serious issue for media industries – minoritised people leave at a faster rate than they enter. As actor and diversity activist Sir Lenny Henry stated starkly at a Department for Culture, Media and Sport select committee: 'At the BBC alone in the last fifteen years there have been twenty-nine initiatives to achieve ethnic diversity, and the numbers are actually going down. Things are being done but they're not really working' (BBC News 2014). This can be due to personalised forms of racial discrimination encountered in the workplace, often understood in terms of 'institutional racism'. But more specific to this manifesto, the version of diversity that focuses on representation/visibility ignores how cultural production – that is, the actual process of making cultural commodities – is a harmful experience for people of colour. This has been the finding of research that has directly studied the experiences of racialised people working in the cultural industries. Examples of these kinds of harms include the burden placed on these individuals to represent their communities, even if their creative/aesthetic practice is not particularly about racial experience. This burden becomes greater when the individual finds that emphasising their racial/ethnic identities (in a way that they may have wanted to avoid) produces higher rewards for labour.

Moreover, despite the economic value placed on diversity, people of colour remain a risky investment for commissioners/executives. As a consequence, cultural producers from under-represented backgrounds are not afforded the same creative freedoms as their white, middle-class counterparts. To mitigate this risk, the very standardised/rationalised production behind the making of cultural commodities like films, books and music steers producers into particular racial characterisations and storylines that are deemed the most commercially viable. This leads to a deeply disturbing scenario where people of colour who work in media, despite their best intentions, or indeed political motivations, can become complicit in the making of racial stereotypes. As an example, the misogyny, homophobia and glamorisation of violence in certain forms of rap music is as much the consequence of industry-established genre convention as it is the individual values of rappers.

Thus, the diversity approach that measures representation in terms of visibility does not address the hostility inside cultural industries. Diversity is merely seen as something to be added to an existing organisational structure, which, in doing so, ensures that the status quo remains intact. As a consequence, we must move beyond a preoccupation with 'representation' that undergirds diversity initiatives, whether in relation to media content or the composition of the creative workforce. Instead, we need to attend to the structural nature of media that makes the cultures of production inside it such a difficult space for racialised people and other under-represented groups. Anti-racist activist work needs to disengage with the issue of representation and instead engage with the project of radically reimagining the very structure of media.

The Limits of Diversity and Representation

The political economy of representation

This manifesto still insists that representation matters. The very importance of media for social justice activism is in how it provides openings where the marginalised can challenge the powerful through representational strategies. If racism is the dehumanisation of those classified as Other, then media and creative/aesthetic practice is a key arena where the Other can restore its humanity (or indeed, bring attention to the racist underpinnings of certain notions of the 'human'). Despite our critique of diversity practice, the logic of diversity has nonetheless opened a space for Black, Brown and Asian people to craft their own media stories that tell of their own experiences. In recent years, we have seen some powerful forms of popular culture that have been made by creators from a range of historically marginalised backgrounds, who have managed to break open a door (or rather have found opportune moments) to enter. These stories have sometimes drawn direct attention to racial injustice (such as Steve McQueen's groundbreaking *Small Axe* series of films that cover significant moments in Black British history). At other times, utilising an array of different aesthetic strategies as well as novel characterisations, Black, Brown and Asian people have destabilised common-sense understandings of race in a more playful fashion (for example, recent television comedy dramas such as *Atlanta*, *I May Destroy You*, *Juice* and *Reservation Dogs*). It is these types of texts that we believe epitomise Stuart Hall's notion of *new ethnicities*, involving articulations of race and ethnicity with class, disability, gender and sexuality, to create new radical depictions of difference and everyday life. In doing so, they refuse and transcend the reductive terms of positive/negative, authentic/stereotypical, truthful/false that typically frame the way that the representation of race in media is understood by audiences, critics and activists.

The point we want to make, however, is that the focus of anti-racist activism needs to be more than just an engagement with debates on whether a particular representation of a racially minoritised group is racist or not. To begin a discussion of where anti-racist activism should be located, it is worth reiterating two main arguments from the previous section. Firstly, as we have stressed, labour and representation need to be taken equally seriously. Yet in doing so we need to reject the simplistic assumption that more diversity in media leads to more diverse content. Instead, we need to be attuned to how cultural production can be harmful to those from marginalised backgrounds, where they experience stricter creative control and have less value attached to their work – related to the lack of value that media ascribe to the communities that they belong to. Secondly, we need to leave behind diversity and its conception of representation as based on visibility and accuracy. Instead, we need a more complex understanding of representation – that it is contingent and always under contestation. The anti-racist aim is not about getting representation right; after all, who is to determine the correct way to represent, for example, Black or Muslim people? Rather, it is about opening representational practices, that is, ensuring that under-represented cultural producers have more autonomy, or at least the same creative freedoms as their white, middle-class, counterparts. In this regard, the focus of anti-racist *activism* should be less on the text, and more on transforming the material conditions of production that shape the way that the text appears. In other words, we call for greater focus on the *political economy of representation*. This entails addressing three areas.

First is corporate power. Media are dominated by a small number of conglomerates where the arrival of tech giants has helped consolidate rather than challenge this power. In music, for instance, just three major record labels dominate nearly two-thirds of the global market: Sony Music Entertainment, Universal Music Group and Warners Music Group. Streaming services such as Spotify and Apple Music have transformed the very economic model of music in largely detrimental ways for music artists who overall make less money from the sale of their music. The few acts who have benefited the most financially from streaming are those already on huge major label deals. Moreover, major label acts secure the most lucrative corporate sponsorship/ branding deals – another increasingly significant revenue stream for musicians as actual record sales plummet. All these gains come at the expense of artists who are not connected to major label networks, who experience precarity, insecurity and low rewards for their labour.

In this context, creators of colour are amongst those who suffer the most. While it would be too simplistic to insist that corporate media stifles creativity – and the most successful corporate executives recognise that audiences demand originality and innovation as much as familiarity and formula – the ultimate pursuit for profit means that alternative, experimental and subversive modes of cultural expression are marginalised due to their perceived lack of commerciality. This has direct ramifications for racialised cultural producers trying to intervene in the production of racial stereotypes. As mentioned, these producers are considered commercially high risk by corporate media and therefore find their access to the biggest production/ promotion budgets and largest distribution net- works blocked. Moreover, corporate media lack racial and ethnic diversity the most, wherein those few Black, Brown and Asian people who find a way in, through a combination of talent, determination, hard work and luck, though ultimately through the patronage of white creative managers, are subjected to what the same white creative managers deem commercial. In this context, corporate production offers less autonomy to people of colour, and places constraints on the stories they want to tell. As stated, it can steer them into reproducing the tired and damaging racial tropes that they had sought to challenge in the first place.

The second area that needs to be addressed is PSM. Public service media exists in many different forms across different socially democratic nations, including different sources of funding. It is a more significant presence in certain nations over others. Considering the global shift towards neoliberalism, PSM has found its power diminished, as it has been forced to compete with commercial media to remain relevant (and funded). It should be recognised as well that PSM, while theoretically independent from the state, has also historically been run by cultural elites, who have used these institutions to maintain their authority and the status quo, which in turn has made PSM an ambivalent space for minoritised groups.

However, the very foundation of PSM is a commitment – in theory at least – to cater for the nation's diverse communities, and to create a coherent source of national community. As a consequence, PSM has historically provided the most professional opportunities for media workers from minoritised backgrounds. In terms of content, before the age of streaming, PSM has been one of the few spaces where audiences would see/hear people from racial/ethnic minority communities. The approach to programming is often shaped by a nation's own approach to multiculturalism, ranging from accommodationist to assimilationist. PSM is one of the few spaces in national media where you would find programmes specifically for certain communities. In recent times, mirroring global trends, the diversity approach has become more dominant, where there is less minority programming (for example, in the 1990s/2000s, the BBC shut down its specialist Afro-Caribbean and Asian Programming Units), and has instead adopted

74

an approach of integrating minority groups into 'mainstream' programming.

While this has meant we see more Black, Brown and Asian faces on our screens than ever before, it also means we learn less about Black, Brown and Asian experience. In light of the reference to how PSM is often run by cultural elites, it has produced similar conditions of production as corporate media. While there is theoretically less emphasis on being commercial (though as mentioned, PSM has had to learn to think more commercially to maintain its value and prestige), Black, Brown and Asian cultural producers working inside PSM have found that the programmes they make are ultimately shaped by the Eurocentric/ethnocentric worldview of predominantly white senior commissioners. Again, research shows that, in the UK at least, the retainment of people from under-represented communities is a major issue for PSM. This compounds a further, broader issue: the failure for PSM to attract young (diverse) audiences, whose cultural consumption has shifted to social media and YouTube in particular.

The third area that demands attention is the sphere of independent media. We include here community media (media made by and for specific communities – often migrant), independent media companies that produce content for national broadcasters/networks, cinema and streaming platforms, and also digital platforms that distribute content made by marginalised groups. Independent media provide the most fertile space for the marginalised, allowing full creative (and political) autonomy. However, it is also characterised by the most insecure and precarious form of creative labour. *gal–dem* (2015–2023) was one of the best-known independent platforms operating out of the UK, a print and online magazine run by women and non-binary people of colour. It became a hugely influential space for communities who have been historically excluded and marginalised by media. Perhaps its most significant impact was in how it influenced 'mainstream' media, in highlighting how these communities not only exist but are at the vanguard of popular culture. *gal–dem* helped these communities accrue value and worth but was framed directly in terms of a social justice programme. In 2023, however, *gal–dem* was forced to close down for financial reasons. The harsh reality for such platforms that want to maintain independence and are wary of corporate co-optation is that they struggle to operate economically, with their workers receiving the lowest rewards for labour.

The Limits of Diversity and Representation

Turning away from diversity

Media are obsessed with diversity. So much of the media we consume today is produced through the logic of diversity. But while we acknowledge that diversity has provided opportunities for creators of colour, the overall tendency is that this has led to a disingenuous post-racial vision of society, which can at worst distract and at best create complacency around the ongoing forms of racial violence, subjugation and economic exploitation that characterise modern societies across the globe. Moreover, media industries remain overwhelmingly white, especially in their upper echelons. Diversity has created a space for the racialised to share their content, but it is *unraced* (i.e., white) dominant culture that profits the most from the diversity turn in media.

Echoing prior work which points this out, we assert that the focus for anti-racist activism should *not* be how to improve the representation of race in media. After all, as Warner (2017) highlights, forms of 'plastic representation' in media do not signify meaningful structural change. Too often, activists and audiences become embroiled in ultimately frivolous debates over whether a certain depiction of a culture or person is authentic or not. More disturbingly, as we shall touch on in the next chapter, these debates become lucrative content for Big Tech companies who use this engagement to build user profiles to sell to advertisers. Rather, as Stuart Hall demonstrated, we understand that the politics of representation is always contingent and always under contestation, or to put it in less academic terms, *always up for grabs*. The task for anti-racist media activism is to transform the political economy of representation, to diffuse corporate power, to build more robust PSM, and to lower the barriers to entry and provide financial support for cultural producers from under-represented communities. The purpose is to create creative, fertile spaces for Black, Brown and Asian cultural producers to tell their stories, whatever they want them to be, whether on issues of race/racism or not; that is, to make media a truly free space.

4

The Dilemmas of Digital Culture

Duality and digital participation

Accounting for the benefits and limitations of forms of digital participation and digital culture, this chapter focuses on the relationship between social media, artificial intelligence (AI), mainstream mass media (MSM) and anti-racist work. Contemporary digital processes, internet trends and content-sharing platforms impact how racism and anti-racism manifests in media contexts and even physical spaces such as protest sites which are policed using facial recognition technology. From constructing threads on X (formerly Twitter) to responding to reels on TikTok – digital participation presents the possibility to forge anti-racist solidarities, cultivate anti-racist consciousness-raising, and connect with anti-racist actions around the world. However, participating in different digital spaces can also expose people to harassment, abuse and datafication processes that are at odds with their safety, values and anti-racism.

Our focus on these matters is not intended to suggest that anti-racism ever solely depends on internet technologies and digital culture. Rather, as digital culture is part of the daily lives of many people and the political activities of many places, a meaningful anti-racist media manifesto must grasp both the potentials and shortcomings of using digital tools as part of anti-racist work. Also, as the days of digital culture existing at the margins of MSM are long gone, it is crucial to understand how internet technologies and trends are implicated in both the racist and anti-racist workings of MSM.

Tackling the duality of digital participation involves dealing with tensions between critical approaches to using digital platforms and the rise of self-branding practices online, both of which can be implicated in ideas about, and experiences of, activism. As such, this chapter reflects on the collision of influencer culture, news media and activism, including related questions about the potential (mis)uses of digital culture to aid anti-racist media and messaging. As journalists are facing the ongoing chilling and deadly effects of state-sanctioned efforts to prohibit anti-racism, anti-coloniality and expressions of solidarity by/with structurally oppressed peoples – such as support for the liberation of Palestine – this chapter particularly focuses on dynamics between digital culture, news media, and work and labour conditions in journalism.

The chapter's broader discussion of digital participation involves recognition of the relationship between structural inequalities, geopolitical power relations and people's (in)access to internet technologies. Oppressed people in colonised and occupied lands today are often denied consistent access to the internet as part of violent governmental efforts to suppress their freedom of speech and prohibit dissenting reporting. This includes disrupting people from publicly naming and challenging genocide – a term that British/Western MSM tiptoes around, if not outright obstructs, in news coverage of Gaza and Palestine more widely.

Accordingly, instead of regarding digital culture as accessible to all, we expressly acknowledge that distinct differences between people's material conditions and societal treatment at local, national and international levels impact who can and cannot participate in various digital spaces, as well as impacting what is at stake when they can or cannot do so. In other words, not everyone can access a stable internet connection and accompanying technologies that enable forms of digital participation, and even when people do, their treatment and monitoring online can considerably vary in ways that reflect racism and its nexus with forms of oppression such as Islamophobia, xenophobia and colourism. Therefore, we consider what this means when working towards an anti-racist media future that supports all oppressed people.

As there are numerous types of digital technology and social media that are used for both racist and anti-racist purposes, it is vital to acknowledge differences between the affordances and limitations of specific platforms that can aid and obstruct anti-racist work. For example, while the micro-blogging focus of Twitter once facilitated real-time and concise written and multimedia coverage of news as it unfolded (previously, in tweets of 140 characters or fewer), since the platform's takeover and rebranding as X by Elon Musk, its legitimacy has been called into question, with critics voicing concerns that the platform now mainly serves to amplify Musk and his equally right-wing supporters. Relatedly, when constructing an anti-racist media manifesto, it is crucial to move beyond utopian framings of the internet, while also exploring the potential for internet technologies to be engaged in ways that enable substantial and collective anti-racist work rather than merely facilitating individualistic and gestural politics.

This chapter details how such digital developments have impacted structurally oppressed people in a range of ways that cannot be comprehended using binary terms such as 'good' and 'bad'. Hence, this work explores experiences of ambivalence and amplification amid forms of anti-racist digital participation. In doing so, it outlines some of the limitations of common 'digital rights' frameworks which are often implicitly positioned as 'post-racial' in nature through their uncritical use of the general concept of 'the citizen'.

The writing that follows responds to key questions concerning anti-racism and media. It considers whether digital developments have resulted in the 'redistribution' of forms of 'power' by reflecting on the digital presence of MSM that is entwined with Big Tech and pressures to self-brand online. Before discussing this in more detail, we outline key elements of the machinations of digital racism. Overall, this chapter pays attention to the dynamics of digital racism and digital anti-racist action, such as how Big Tech operates in ways that reflect and maintain racism. While we acknowledge beneficial dimensions of digital culture and we refuse fatalistic framings of it, our manifesto points to the importance of analogue media in anti-racist futures. Challenging the capitalist-oriented 'pivot to video', 'death of print' and 'clickbait' ethos of MSM, we argue that an anti-racist media future may revitalise analogue activities and slower media practices.

Digital racism

Although racism is not the result of digital culture, it occurs in ways that are distinctly shaped by it. In July 2021, not long after a surge in British discourse about racism and BLM, the final of the UEFA European Football Championship 2020 was followed by racist online abuse directed at England football team players Marcus Rashford, Jadon Sancho and Bukayo Saka. Soon after, there was much public and political discussion of digital racism and how to tackle it. Recent responses to the issue of online abuse include the UK Parliament's Online Safety Bill, which features a section on racist abuse and includes the Euro 2020 final as a case study. Prior to that, charity Glitch reported on 'COVID-19 and the Epidemic of Online Abuse', emphasising that 'Black and minoritised women and non-binary people were almost as likely to be abused based on ethnicity as they were to be abused based on gender' (Glitch 2020: 22). Since then, and echoing impactful Black feminist work on the intersections of racism, sexism and misogyny, known as misogynoir (Bailey 2021), Glitch (2023) released 'The Digital Misogynoir Report', which focuses on working to end the 'dehumanising of Black women on social media'.

As is highlighted by previous and extensive research and work, misogynoir occurs online in many ways that involve forms of misinformation, disinformation and abuse (Harry 2021). Shafiqah Hudson's creation of the hashtag #YourSlipIsShowing, and the surrounding Black feminist work to address misogynoir online, brought vital attention to the prevalence of coordinated online accounts pretending to be Black women while harassing and abusing real Black women (Hampton 2019). Put briefly, digital racism and its entanglement with other forms of oppression is rife. Yet, in the context of the UK, apart from a small number of organisations such as Glitch, digital rights efforts to address harassment and abuse often avoid indepth discussion of how racism, sexism, misogyny and other interconnected forms of oppression are implicated in online experiences and the extent to which a person is likely to be deemed a citizen, and, even, a human with rights. Digital platforms and

internet technologies are impacted by racial capitalism (McMillan Cottom 2021) – how racism impacts the construction and accumulation of forms
of capital, such as the value that society attaches to
people, products, places and processes. So, pursuing anti-racist work with the use of various digital
platforms and internet technologies is not without
its obstacles.

Many online content-sharing and social media
sites are designed and governed in ways that contrast with the objectives of anti-racist organisers,
who may face censorship, abuse and sanctions
when attempting to post anti-racist messages and
share related resources online. Also, the digital
work of anti-racist organisers can be exposed to
the potential of being commodified and co-opted
by commercial organisations that pursue forms of
profit by performing a palatable proximity to certain anti-racist movements.

In response to demand for viral social media content and evidence of the social values of brands, some
commercial organisations attempt to leverage the language of anti-racism and associated online hashtags
in ways that can benefit them but may distract from
and distort the realities of anti-racist work. The contradictions of the internet and the constrained yet
promising potential of countercultural discourse in

digital spheres has been illuminated as part of essential research on the possibilities and limitations related to activism online (Jackson, Bailey and Foucault Welles 2020). Impacted by various internet technologies, digital culture is best understood as being a collage of different apps, platforms, sites, identities, senses and interactions that are digitally mediated. Cognisant of that, when focusing on the dynamic between racism and digital culture, we account for how the functions of specific digital spaces and processes reflect, reinforce and respond to racism.

Essentially, we ask: *what elements of digital culture enable or challenge racism?* Although a lengthy answer to this question is beyond the scope of our manifesto, this chapter tackles some of the many aspects of digital culture that are entwined with racist media and anti-racist media. While considering this, we focus on examples related to local journalism and storytelling, AI, social media sites, and the self-branding pressures and practices of media professionals online.

Digital culture meets mainstream media

Since the turn of the new millennium, internet technologies and digital culture have become part of the everyday existence of many people. Long gone are the times of digital culture being perceived as a niche or underground world that only hackers, cyber-sleuths and other information technology experts inhabit. Now, digital culture is mainstream.

While there are still subcultures within it and 'hidden' parts of the internet such as the dark web, digital culture has moved from the periphery of society to the centre. Examples of this include media brands establishing a social media presence and the corporate capture of user-generated content (e.g., memes) by fandom communities. While digital culture is diverse and includes the grassroots work of anti-racist organisers, the powerful force of social media algorithms (Birhane 2022; Noble 2018) impacts whether digital content is amplified online or is suppressed and censored. Accordingly, an anti-racist media future must grapple with how to ensure that the digital efforts of anti-racist organisers are not obstructed by the workings of Big Tech.

Although news coverage and popular culture are distinguished in our chapters, digital culture has blurred the boundaries between both – from the 'memeification' of political stories to the inclusion of social media posts in televised news. This means that when we reflect on how racism manifests in digital culture, it is crucial to also contend with the changing and overlapping norms of both news coverage *and* popular culture. Such norms include audiences being encouraged to use specific hashtags and social media sites to share thoughts and questions with MSM, including by tagging news anchors in their posts, which may then be responded to by those representatives of MSM brands.

As digital culture has expanded opportunities for audiences to speak to, and with, MSM, it has also challenged exclusionary notions of journalism and cultural production, by bringing attention to local, freelance and grassroots forms of such work, which exist beyond the confines of corporate media institutions. The ability to publicly respond to MSM and/or to broadcast yourself online is not innately anti-racist or pro–local journalism and cultural production. However, such ability has provided the opportunity for people from historically oppressed groups to amplify issues, news and work that concerns them, and in ways that bring attention to a diversity of media and cultural expression that is seldom embraced by MSM. This is all with the caveat that online communication can be fragile, as it is subject to oppressive Big Tech and state interventions.

While there are differences between news coverage and popular culture, both were impacted by society's move away from a one-to-many broadcast model that typified much media in the twentieth century. The internet technologies and digital culture of recent decades have enabled more dialogic forms of media and communications. This means that in the absence of meaningful coverage by MSM, people have relatively autonomously turned to digital tools that enable them to record, report on and broadcast news related to racism and the lives of people who are targeted by it. For example, digital storytelling – including multilingual media – has played a pivotal part in forms of grassroots and community journalism that reach a broad, even global, audience. However, without the financial and material resources to enable and sustain such work, anti-racist digital storytelling and local journalism are often at risk of being one-off or short-term in nature, limiting their potentially transformative impact and their ability to connect with people further afield too.

Although transnational anti-racist organising occurred long before the emergence of the internet, the development of the digital cultures that are part of it has contributed to contemporary approaches to anti-racist organising across and within different countries. Particularly as many governments around the world attempt to prohibit people's rights to protest in-person, digital spaces have played an increasingly significant role in forms of dissent, resistance and protest action. Also, due to online functions that can enable the relatively rapid translation of text into different languages, digital platforms can facilitate solidarity-building between communities in different countries. An example of impactful anti-racist work that draws on digital culture but does not depend on it is the European Race and Imagery Foundation (ERIF), who 'are positioned specifically in a bid to depart from US-centric understandings of race and racism, which do not always necessarily relate to the European experience'.

ERIF highlight one of many reasons why visual media can be a powerful force that simultaneously enables racism and anti-racism, defining imagery as 'both the tangible expression of views and ideas that people have as well as imaginary spaces and their material consequences, such as the lived experiences of racial discrimination' (European Race and Imagery Foundation 2023). In the context of digital culture, such imagery is impacted by a wide range of technologies and trends. These include the rise of AI and computer-generated imagery (CGI) models/influencers, who, despite not being real people, are visual creations that are constructed and personified in distinctly racialised and gendered ways.

AI/CGI models/influencers, who have high numbers of social media followers and partner with brands to boost their campaigns, are seldom racialised as white, highlighting the market appeal of malleable and imagined forms of racial difference. As the number of brands using such AI/CGI models/influencers increases, so too does critique of the potential for these creations to be strategically used to portray brands as racially diverse and inclusive. Thus, an anti-racist media future that challenges superficial notions of racial diversity must include work that is attuned to the potential for media corporations to leverage AI/CGI creations to project shallow images of them as anti-racist.

In addition to tackling that, an anti-racist media future must be alert to how governments and political entities strategically engage real people who are influencers, to aid their messaging and, even, propaganda. The following headline in *The Washington Post* exemplifies influencer culture's weaponisation as part of geopolitics, such as via tourism-centred portrayals of places (Fullerton 2022). Clearly, an anti-racist media future must be one that critically addresses invocations of influencer culture that aid oppressive actions, including sectarianism and xenophobia which intersect with racism.

To address the role of digital culture in both racism and anti-racism, it is essential to understand the power of visual culture more broadly. ERIF's (2023) explanation of how visual imagery can function provides a key outline of the power of representations of race in the media:

Imagery can be employed to either renew or (re)produce conventions of racist representation and it can justify violence and the disciplining of people of colour. However, imagery can also be employed to oppose racism and renew traditions of resistance against racism. In this case, imagery provides space to breathe and heal, and open pathways to imagine more just futures.

As the work of ERIF demonstrates, in the fight for an anti-racist world, visual culture and media remain key domains that have been contested and which have been shaped by digital developments in recent decades.

Much of digital culture's emphasis on speed, immediacy and virality results in the rapid creation and sharing of content. At times, this can aid urgent anti-racist messaging and its powerful reach, such as when denouncing the genocidal actions of governments. However, much of digital culture's focus on rapid responses and sound-bite style content can fuel forms of misinformation and disinformation that bolster racist propaganda. The development of 'deep fake' audios and videos, and of various forms of AI/CGI digital media, has complicated necessary fact-checking processes by blurring lines between what is real and what is artificial. Therefore, an anti-racist media future must be invested in working to collectively equip people with fact-checking and critical media skills that address the prevalence of multimedia content and social media posts that present false information as fact.

The twenty-first-century arrival of wireless internet access and devices such as laptops and smartphones marked a shift in how people could experience media, at home, when at school and work, and while on the move. As has been emphasised, what followed was a flurry of social media and content-sharing sites such as Facebook, Instagram, X (formerly known as Twitter) and YouTube, contributing to how audiences could talk – or tweet and video blog (vlog) – back at TV presenters, journalists and media critics. This ushered in the emergence of digital media punditry and media industry jobs that focused squarely on online content and specific social media sites. But what that also meant was the increased exposure of media professionals to public abuse and harassment, including racism online.

Despite it often being deemed a more open, inclusive and alternative space than the MSM industry (e.g., TV, film, print press), digital culture is rife with forms of racism and is a broad culture that is often interwoven with MSM rather than serving as a departure from it. AI has been at the centre of much contemporary public discourse on power and internet technologies, raising questions about the humanness of digital culture and how inequalities are implicated in it. However, much moral panic about AI does not tackle how AI affects work and labour conditions, both within and beyond MSM. Tending to such matters, we consider what role, if any, AI might play in an anti-racist media future.

AI, inequalities and work

We are at a point in time when forms of AI are frequently, and often frantically, commented on in MSM. Such contemporary commentary on AI includes coverage of a campaign featuring an AI-generated hypothetical candidate – Hope Sogni – for the role of tenth president of FIFA, the international governing body of association football.

Symbolising the sense of spectacle that can surround the hypervisibility of people of colour in the media – who in this case are simply computer-generated, the controversial AI creation was framed as being a Black woman. It was developed with the use of generative AI to enable it to respond to questions and was intended to point out sexism and misogyny in football – notably, a focus on their intersections with racism seemed to be sidelined. As such, Hope Sogni reveals much about media and intersecting power relations, not just football.

The AI creation of Hope Sogni and the wider world of gendered and racialised AI models illuminates some of the complex ways that digital technology is entangled with commentaries on, *and* manifestations of, structural inequalities. The expanding AI industry has sparked many concerns about forms of fakery and data-mining used when generating AI creations that resemble real people. Hence, it is unsurprising that 'authentic' was declared Merriam-Webster's Word of the Year in 2023, reflecting intensified societal interest in who and what is perceived as genuine and real, including in the context of media.

Arguably, the term 'authentic' is simply a label that is used to describe people and entities in ways that idealise them within dominant systems of value (e.g., their potential to yield capital in monetary terms). The focus on 'authenticity' in much discourse in 2023 follows on from the previous buzzword status of 'post-truth' – an Oxford Dictionaries Word of the Year in 2016, in response to past discourse about (un)trustworthiness, the US election and Britain's referendum on exiting the European Union (Brexit). Society continues to grapple with ideas about 'authenticity' and truth in increasingly mediated ways which are shaped by changes to digital technology and online trends, as well as being impacted by racism.

Too much media discourse about AI and related questions about 'authenticity' involve AI being referred to as some sort of abstract force that exists independently of the work, decisions and other actions of people. This can result in organisations strategically separating discourse on AI from collective struggles related to workers' rights, including within and across industries and different roles, such as forms of media creation, content moderation and data-mining. In addition to AI having the potential to put the livelihoods of some media industry workers at risk, including by replicating their likeness and the likeness of their work in extractive and non-consensual ways, the AI industry itself typically depends on the exploited work of people, particularly those who are not white. Hence, AI can play a pivotal role in the reinforcement of racism, and not only due to its potential to yield media content that features racist depictions and discourse.

In an article for Noema magazine, focusing on the experiences of people who annotate and label data that AI depends on, Adrienne Williams, Milagros Miceli and Timnit Gebru (2022) bring attention to 'The Exploited Labor behind Artificial Intelligence':

> Companies make sure to hire people from poor and underserved communities, such as refugees, incarcerated people and others with few job options, often hiring them through third party firms as contractors rather than as full time employees. While more employers should hire from vulnerable groups like these, it is unacceptable to do it in a predatory manner, with no protections.

Any anti-racist media future that is invested in addressing work and labour conditions is a future that must include a focus on addressing the exploited work and labour conditions of the groups of people that Williams et al. (2022) highlight, whose repetitive data-annotating and other AI-related work is typically regarded as existing separately to the media industry, despite it being clearly interconnected. An anti-racist media future must move beyond merely focusing on AI media representations (e.g., Hope Sogni), to address and improve the work and labour conditions of precarious data workers – whose work shapes forms of AI that are increasingly a part of the media industry, and who are often people impacted by racism, xenophobia and other inter-related forms of oppression. This is not to suggest that an anti-racist media future is pro-AI. Rather, it is a future that affirms connections between the work and labour struggles of Black, Brown, and other racially oppressed people, who have jobs in different yet interrelated sectors.

An anti-racist media future is one that must also involve the media industry moving beyond sim-plistic celebrations versus moral panic positions in response to digital culture. This must include acknowledging that AI is here to stay, and then looking critically at the way that racial capital-ism shapes both the media industry and forms of AI-related data-mining. One of many ways that media organisations can support this approach is by aiding and engaging with in-depth, independ-ent, long-term and critical research, to be informed about: (1) the changing landscape of internet technologies and the affordances of specific digital platforms; (2) the forms of power and intersect-ing inequalities that are inextricably implicated in the design and governance of such technologies and platforms; and (3) what media organisations and the industry at large can do to facilitate and bolster changes that challenge such forms of oppression.

Digital presence, pressures and protections

Anti-racist action can involve critically calling out nation states, dominant ideologies, and political parties and affiliated figures, resulting in significant backlash from racist individuals and institutions who seek to intimidate, harm and even kill anti-racists. The abuse aimed at anti-racists online must be understood as always connected to offline settings, where anti-racists may face physical violence and forms of political persecution that can result in their incarceration or, in some cases, their state-sanctioned annihilation. This means that the online surveillance of anti-racists and the collective organisations that they are part of can quite literally be a matter of life or death(s).

As well as generating digitally mediated ways to connect, co-ordinate and commune, the internet and some of the many digital platforms and processes that it has yielded contribute to the surveillance and targeting of anti-racist activists and journalists. Digital racism does not exist in isolation from issues such as digital sexism and misogynistic abuse. Again, owing to misogynoir (Bailey 2021; Glitch 2023), the digital presence, work and activism of Black women is often responded to in ways that include relentless and vitriolic forms of harassment and abuse. So, media organisations' expectations that Black women make themselves visible and accessible online can amount to pressures that push Black women to develop a digital presence in a way that may be at odds with their safety, support and protection.

While many journalists and other media workers face pressures to self-brand online, Black journalists can face a distinctly racialised pressure to become an influencer or establish a high-profile presence on social media to be deemed worthy of interest from white editors and predominantly white MSM. In turn, such journalists may encounter implicit expectations that they are visibly present on certain platforms despite the digital racism and interconnected forms of oppression that they may be a target of. Relatedly, an anti-racist media future must involve media organisations working in ways that more actively account for, and aim to mitigate and address, the racism that their employees face.

We argue that many media organisations may need to reconsider their current expectations of the digital presence and online practices of their employees, to avoid forcing workers to participate in digital spaces that can cause them harm.

Put differently, media organisations must ensure that such expectations of their employees' digital presence are accompanied by provision of substantial support and protections to address the reality that Black, Asian and other people who are targets of racism offline are also targets of it online. Such protections could include providing employees with the right to propose their own preferred approach to the construction or intentional absence of their digital presence, rather than presenting them with a standardised organisational policy that typically fails to meaningfully address digital racism and other interconnected forms of abuse. Therefore, we call on organisations to reflect on the specifics of their social media policy – if they have one – to ensure that it does not prevent employees from calling out racism online, should they wish to do so, and to ensure that it enables employees' agency in relation to their digital participation. We regard aiding the online autonomy and support of Black, Asian and other media workers who face racism to be one of several key approaches that industry organisations should pursue if they are truly committed to an anti-racist media future.

Digital culture is no solution to racism

Continuing conversations about transforming the political economy of media, this chapter has reflected on internet technologies and their entanglements with the media industry, work and labour conditions, and forms of racism and anti-racism. Consequently, the manifesto proposals in this chapter build on those identified in the previous ones, by outlining crucial ways that digital culture can be both embraced and critiqued as part of moves towards an anti-racist media.

When tackling racism at a national or global scale, anti-racist organisers often find themselves working in ways that must be sensitive to the specifics of their immediate surroundings, such as when responding to local racist incidents and institutions. Mindful of this, it is important that our manifesto accounts for how racism and anti-racism are shaped by the specifics of different geopolitical contexts, meaning that no matter how general our manifesto is, its application must be tailored to different regions and countries, where the demographics of who is the target of racism can vary, as can the affordances and norms of digital platforms.

Digital culture is certainly far from being democratised, but elements of digital culture can be engaged to challenge hierarchical MSM industry dynamics that have historically been steeped in societal racism, classism, ableism, sexism, Islamophobia and other intersecting oppressions. Facets of digital culture that continue to lend themselves to anti-racist work include modes of multimedia, multilingual and grassroots storytelling, which warrant much more and consistent public funding, such as to support forms of anti-racist news and storytelling specifically by and/or for children and young people. After all, the future is an undoubtedly intergenerational one, so people of all ages must be supported in their efforts to strive towards an anti-racist media environment, and an overall anti-racist world.

5

Towards an
Anti-Racist Media

In the real world

One could read all of this and say, oh look, the academics are at it again. Serenely insulated from the pressures of everyday professional routines and volatile industrial dynamics, they call on the media to implement their theoretical and political preferences, as if ideas walk in straight lines. And by issuing a manifesto, no less – we have interpreted the world, now the point is for you to change it. Fair enough, up to a point; the tension between theory and practice, though often overstated, is thorny enough on this terrain. And yet, any retreat to a comforting dichotomy of real world and ivory tower neglects an implacable reality. Marginalised audiences, whenever they are asked about media, consistently point to problems of misrepresentation, sensationalist and partial coverage, and patterns of invisibility and exclusion. Further, they recognise that these are structural problems.

To underline this reality, one further example from the realm of news coverage. A 2023 report by the Reuters Institute for the Study of Journalism argued forcefully for the need for news producers to take seriously the detrimental impacts of misrepresentation and under-representation on marginalised communities. Based on extensive qualitative research with disadvantaged and racialised groups in Brazil, India, the UK and the US, the report details similar patterns of frustration with relentless negativity, unfair treatment, harmful stereotyping and inadequate attention. Strikingly, the report underlines how respondents

> highlight in concrete terms the impact that inaccurate and inadequate representation in news coverage can have on the lives of people belonging to marginalized and other communities distant and disconnected from those parts of society that are privileged and powerful. While some of the critiques raised in this report will sound familiar to many journalists, the deeply personal stakes articulated here, which involve potential for profound harms, ought to lead some to reflect on whether their own organisations' commitments to these matters are

duly aligned with the urgency of the problems as perceived by many in the communities we have focused on here (Argeudas et al. 2023: 4).

These findings are replicated in studies of 'diverse' representation in entertainment, and in racialised experiences of social media participation. What underpins the reflections of these audiences and users is a pronounced sense that much media simply does not imagine and address a public that meaningfully and fully includes them. Much work, evidently, needs to be done to transform this, and it must happen in practices, policy and systemic change. This manifesto argues that change will remain superficial unless media institutions commit to thinking about race and racism as oppressive structures that they are always implicated in, sometimes productive of, but also often in a position to challenge and oppose.

The manifest alienation of publics suggests that an anti-racist media future need not remain an abstract concept. Instead, it is a vision that can be realised by understanding that media transformation must involve rooting anti-racist commitments and clear transformative goals at different levels of media activity and organisation. Or, perhaps, it is more accurate to describe it as a series of visions, given that thinking about media transformation must encompass both reformist orientations and more radical impulses. We need to identify practices emerging in the current conjuncture that will make things less bad or somewhat better, while also advancing ideas for how media systems can be dis-integrated from the roots and routes of structural racism.

More and better diversity?

On a very basic level, an anti-racist media needs to stop being so white and include more people from different racialised and marginalised backgrounds in its workforce, across the news media and popular entertainment industries. Moreover, this active diversification needs to be ensured at each level of a media organisation, including at the very top, and not concentrated in the lower-paid roles as is the case right now. Given contemporary coordinates of reaction, this goal can be easily dismissed as 'identity politics'. However, even when this criticism is well intentioned, it has little to say about why publics continually point to the importance of *particular forms of identification* in combating misrepresentation and working for more and better representation.

Audience research makes clear that media diversification is a stage in a process of addressing systematic misrecognition and abandonment, not an essentialist end in itself. The Reuters Institute for the Study of Journalism study presented wide-ranging qualitative evidence of how their research participants connected hiring 'more journalists who better reflect the communities they serve' with the possibility of more complete and complex coverage and a better understanding of the distinct needs of – internally – diverse communities (Argeudas et al. 2023: 32). More diversification of the news process is linked to the possibility of better practices; journalists who might have deeper connections or credibility with marginalised communities, who can provide more local and historical context, and who are far less likely to produce narrow and stereotypical coverage. We can apply the same logic to entertainment.

This processual and speculative investment in diversification, therefore, is focused on mitigating media's reproduction of systemic racism. It contrasts starkly with the dominant paradigm of 'diversity' which informs how mainstream media tackle issues of racial inequality. Mainstream media deliberately employ the soft language of diversity to bury the difficult and unforgiving language of racism. Diversity discourse obfuscates the forms of structural and institutional racism that shape media with detrimental effects for workers and audiences.

Dominant approaches to diversity do not provide the tools to address the different types of racial discrimination that exist within media organisations, whether direct forms of racist abuse and denigration, or the way that, in a profit-obsessed industry, people defined by their race and the work they produce are seen as a risky investment. This persistent pattern helps explain why racial stereotyping and forms of misrepresentation persist in news and entertainment media. The hegemonically white perspective of mainstream media will always lean towards the reproduction of racial 'common sense' that it understands mainstream (i.e., white) audiences will recognise. The inclusion of more people of colour in advertisements does little to disrupt this, however much the right might huff about 'over-representation'.

This is why meaningful diversification is critical to the seeding and flourishing of new practices, a modest if important goal. Our discussion of journalism and objectivity, for example, detailed how debates about declining trust in the mainstream presents media with a choice between doubling down on the probity of frayed practices, or exploring how credibility and relevance with complex publics can be established through creative approaches. Lewis Raven Wallace discusses in *The View from Somewhere* how the dichotomy of objectivity and activism that journalists from marginalised backgrounds are faced with obscures how independent, accurate and ethical journalism does not at all depend on policing the presumptive detachment of individual journalists. Contesting objectivity has driven new practices of building trust with publics, where 'transparency, equity, an analysis of power and oppression, and community accountability are all elements of the movement to revive and revise journalism for the twenty-first century' (2019: 13).

It is only through sustained diversification that journalism can begin to cultivate the practices that do justice to the constitution and complexity of multicultural publics, that can challenge the assumptions and frames that mainstream media routinely reproduce, and can 'build trust' by, as a basic requirement, reporting 'all the news that makes a difference, turning media institutions into platforms for reform rather than for the maintenance of a status quo that has long turned a blind eye to systemic forms of injustice' (Zelizer et al. 2021: 98).

The Anti-Racist Media Manifesto

Beyond journalism, diversification can also amount to more than a set of limited representational gestures in entertainment media. Critical to any efforts to bring about an anti-racist media is the enabling of the creative freedom of marginalised groups so they can tell stories they want to tell, whatever ways they want to tell them. Achieving this requires widening and ultimately unsettling the regime of representation that continues to produce patterns of invisibility and hypervisibility, stereotypes and reductive representation.

In chapter 3 we called into the question diversity's sole focus on recruitment, where diversity is seen as an *added extra* to existing structures, rather than a radical transformation of those structures. Nonetheless, there is no avoiding the fact that media need to deliver on promises of more diverse recruitment. At a minimum, more diversity at the decision-making levels of media work will help the experience of workers from marginalised backgrounds. We should stress that transformations in media representation are not guaranteed just because there is a Black or Asian person in charge (just look at the Conservative government in power in Britain in 2024). However, greater diversity in key creative management roles can help transform what Timothy Havens (2013) calls 'industry lore' around what types of Black cultural production are considered valuable, and commercially valuable.

For instance, Shonda Rhimes – one of the few Black women showrunners working in American television – through her globally successful production *Bridgerton*, has managed to challenge the industry lore that English period dramas cannot feature people of colour for the reason that their presence would dispel the authenticity of the piece. While we have reservations about the colour-blind casting that Rhimes has become famous for, which feeds into forms of 'plastic representation' (Warner 2017), it is nonetheless significant that a Black woman has been able to transform dominant industry assumptions in this way.

The fact is that the forms of soft positive action that diversity policy relies on do not cut it. The media industries remain overwhelmingly white. This is owing to two broad reasons. The first is racist and discriminatory employment practices within an industry anyway characterised by precarious employment (which impacts significantly on the class profile of media workers). While media will shy away from this kind of direct assessment, their acceptance that 'unconscious biases' can disadvantage people from marginalised backgrounds provides a stitch that can be unpicked.

The second is that, within marginalised communities themselves, there is a lack of awareness and often distrust of the mainstream media industry as a potential area of work and creative possibility. Statements on job adverts that encourage applications by people from under-represented groups are ineffective since equality law in many countries prevents any kind of positive discrimination, that is, hiring someone based on their ethnic/racial identity. Even in those nations that have historically used affirmative action, these policies are in retreat following powerful attacks from the right, and a tepid defence from the liberal left.

Therefore, we can see no way other than a first step in making media less racist through the adoption of forms of affirmative action. If media understand that they lack meaningful diversity, and that this is a key factor in the ongoing alienation of publics, then these types of policies will enable media organisations to recruit more 'diversely' in a way that they have fundamentally failed to do so far.

As an example of how this can work, in the UK, the organisation Creative Access has used a loophole in UK equality law that allows affirmative action to be enacted for work placements (though not paid work). This has provided opportunities for thousands of young people from mostly racially minoritised backgrounds to get experience in media, including in the biggest media organisations.[1] The American media scholar Darnell Hunt has suggested that media industries employ the 'Rooney Rule': a strategy that has been applied in American sports recruitment, entailing an obligation to shortlist at least one candidate from a racial/ethnic minority background when hiring head coaches and other senior positions.

Forms of affirmative action and positive discrimination are blunt instruments. They do not address the forms of racial discrimination and inequality that media workers will encounter once inside media, and nor will they automatically produce transformative practices that speak to alienated publics. Nonetheless, if an anti-racist media future minimally requires a media that at least reflects the diversity of publics, it an important first step. One that needs ultimately to be coupled with more radical measures.

Confronting the far-right media ecology

The problem of corporate concentration and inequalities in media power is a democratic problem, and one which intensifies the hold and reach of structural racism. In systems where news is primarily a commodity in an intensely competitive media environment, racism is tried-and-tested content, pumped out and primed for enjoyment, pitting some shards of a fragmented public against Others. If, as our colleagues in *The Media Manifesto* remind us, concentrated media power results in media systems failing to provide citizens with 'accurate, diverse and representative media that is capable of informing and nourishing the kind of inclusive public debate that is the lifeblood of functioning democracies' (Fenton et al. 2020: 101), the consequences of this are exacerbated for those racialised as not-quite-citizens.

The enduring problem of spectacular racism-for-profit in the right-wing press and 'partisan' television channels is in the process of being exacerbated by further concentration. The situation in the UK, discussed at the end of chapter 2, is paralleled in many other contexts, where an established reactionary press is moving further to the right in search of the stuff of outraged enjoyment; this dynamic is compounded by takeovers and convergences; and the wider digital ecology provides an endless stream of 'woke and anti-woke' content to satisfy the accelerated news cycle, and the incessant opinion production which provides such a cheap alternative to actual news-gathering.

The question, then, is what does balance mean in media systems that are becoming dangerously unbalanced? There is a clear need for countervailing forms of power that intervene at different levels of media activity. The first is journalistic. Journalists must refuse to legitimate the swathe of far-right ideological outlets that not only present themselves as 'pluralist' news alternatives, but which seek to normalise their operations through increasingly conducting some rudimentary forms of institution-alised journalism. However, doing this simply by hewing to professional norms of neutrality and balance is inadequate to the threat. It is not enough simply to refuse their legitimacy as source material or agenda-setters. An anti-racist sensibility demands critical self-reflection on how, for example, the mainstream coverage of 'immigration' and other racialised issues has provided a fertile discursive space for the newcomers to stake their claim to journalistic authority. Consequently, coverage must be actively countervailing, squeezing out this ideological rent-seeking.

There is a critical need for unions to revitalise their anti-racist activity and orient it to a context in which the nature of the far right, and of far-right discourse, has changed. Supremacist, racist and conspiratorial discourse is far more likely to be articulated in mainstream broadcast by an invited cast of urbane contrarians, 'independent' journalists and ideological entrepreneurs as by the leaders of far-right parties that unions had a historical role in 'no-platforming'. Unions have anti-fascist and anti-racist legacies that can be activated and adapted for a threat that does not stand still. Workers can protest the platforming of discourse that targets the identities and communities of racialised media workers, they can agitate for editorial policies that recognise the contemporary shifts in how racism is expressed. Similarly, journalists and media workers can put pressure on regulatory authorities to intervene in the trend of channels that cosplay as news while pumping out reactionary opinion. In France Reporters without Borders, for example, has pursued the *Autorité de regulation de la communication audiovisuelle et numérique* (ARCOM) to investigate the Bolloré group's Cnews for neglecting its legal obligations to the 'pluralism and independence of information' (Reporters sans Frontières 2024).

And more must be done in many contexts to support media workers where their institutions are bought and merged to groups with a proven record of hard-right political alignment and racism-for-profit.

In 2023, journalists at *Le Journal du Dimanche* went on strike for forty days to oppose the appointment of an openly far-right editor following the paper's takeover by the Bolloré group and left *en masse* once the strike ended. Their struggle demonstrates that journalists do not have to accept the concerted radical-right shift under way in different media systems. Public campaigns have a role to play in supporting this objective and can and should be expanded. The UK-based campaign Stop Funding Hate, and the France-based campaign Sleeping Giants, for example, organise to pressure brands[2] to stop placing advertising in far-right-adjacent sites, or newspapers that profit from anti-migrant scapegoating, or programmes that seek ratings through platforming the far right.

Media and platform racism

The media industry can become complicit in perpetuating online racism and oppression if it does not establish ways to ethically use social media, such as by identifying anti-racist principles to inform organisations' use of platforms and their creation of staff social media use policies. Much mainstream media, public and political discourse on social media ethics tends to overlook how the design and functions of social media sites can be shaped by racism. While we emphasise the importance of online hate speech and racism being actively addressed, such efforts to tackle this must tend to both the *design of* and *material produced on* such sites.

In so doing, it becomes clear that there is no easy straightforward approach to racism on social media. The amplification of right-wing and racist discourse on X following Musk's takeover resulted in many individuals and institutions issuing public statements about their decision to leave the site. In contrast, many often marginalised folks stayed, while affirming years of critique voiced by Black and other racially minoritised people who consistently pointed out that it was never a 'safe' site for all. Writing on such matters for *Wired*, and reiterating insights from Black media and digital studies work, Jason Parham (2023) captures this with the pithy headline: 'Black Twitter Remains Unbothered in Elon Musk's X'.

This ambivalence underlines the importance of media organisations striking a balance between trying to use social media ethically but without disengaging from platforms in ways that may simply shield them from public critique rather than yield anti-racist actions. There can be power in forms of media disengagement (Amponsah 2023), but exiting social media is not an innately ethical or anti-racist decision. In other words, decisions about how the media industry makes use of social media must be informed by anti-racist principles, such as a focus on the collective good rather than the protection and projection of the image and reputation of a single media organisation.

Media organisations must carefully consider whether decisions to turn away from various online sites stem from commitments to ethical values or an effort to absolve them of expectations that they publicly speak up on racism and injustice. We must move beyond a framing of so-called 'good' and 'bad' social media sites. Instead, what is required is the continued challenging of corporate power. This means refusing an 'out of sight, out of mind' mentality that privileges disengaging from individual sites and platforms while doing little to tackle the corporate powers behind them.

That is to say, cultivating media anti-racism requires challenging the role of powerful tech companies in reinforcing oppression. While our vision of an anti-racist media future is of one where tech giants are held accountable, we are also mindful of the limitations of reformist approaches to addressing the structural harms and force of 'Big Tech'. If tech giants originate from a system that produces and sustains inequalities, perhaps for an anti-racist media future to truly be realised, tech giants must cease to exist? In other words, is it possible to imagine a world in which corporate social media on this scale and in this model does not further structural racism?

Regardless, the reality of current conditions endures, and anti-racist media work must broaden to address the problems presented by algorithms and AI. Abeba Birhane (2021) highlights that '[w]hen algorithmic injustice and harm are brought to the fore, most of the solutions on offer (1) revolve around technical solutions and (2) do not center disproportionally impacted communities'. Mitigating the racist design, use and effects of various algorithms and forms of AI is a critical priority, and currently there are crucial examples of collective efforts to tackle these issues, such as the Distributed AI Research Institute (DAIR), 'a space for independent, community-rooted AI research, free from Big Tech's pervasive influence'. We echo their call for more independent research that can feed into disrupting the harms of AI technology while also imagining how such technologies can 'cultivate spaces to accelerate imagination and creation of new technologies and tools to build a better future'.

Anti-racist pluralism

Ideas of pluralism have historically been invoked to describe and prescribe the institutional diversity of the public sphere, a diversity held to map onto the positions and identities that comprise national societies. Although we are critical that this notion has rarely reckoned with the fact that racialised and marginalised communities have been excluded from this vision, the appropriation of this minimally democratic idea to further the circulation of racist discourse requires a response.

What, then, would a meaningfully anti-racist pluralism require? In a way, this involves us going back to the future – how can the modern media institutions, vested in pluralism and democratisation but also complicit in reproducing the 'white nation', be reformed and transformed? What forms of systemic reconstruction can dilute the flows of racist discourse, increase meaningful diversification and build structures that do not reproduce structural racism?

Pluralism does not merely happen, it is constructed and cultivated. Critical to the development of a more democratic and egalitarian media that works for the benefit of minoritised communities is enacting significant media reform. This entails anti-racists becoming a more active presence in existing media reform campaigns. Such movements have not always foregrounded issues of racial justice in their campaigning. This is often a consequence of the assumption that more robust media regulation will automatically lead to better outcomes for marginalised groups like racialised minorities, as well as women and LGBTQ+ groups.

More anti-racist activist involvement in media reform campaigns can work to integrate consciousness of systemic racism to challenges to the current shape of the media system. The involvement of anti-racist activists in media reform campaigns can help build the movement for a more free, equal and open media, at least in part by demonstrating how the reproduction of racism is dependent on the key problems targeted by media reform campaigning.

Central to this is support for more robust forms of regulation designed to break up media monopolies. Although these are not immediately applicable internationally, the policy initiatives of the UK's Media Reform Coalition[3] suggest important lines of mobilisation: (1) breaking up private monopolies when they have too much control over a particular market; (2) ensuring internal independence and plurality in the largest media organisations; and (3) supporting more diverse voices with new funding and ownership models. From an anti-racist perspective, one of the main aims of breaking up media monopolies is to enable independent media production run by racial and ethnic minoritised groups.

By independent media we are referring to a range of forms, from community media – media made by and for specific communities – independent media companies that produce content for national broadcasters, networks, cinema and streaming platforms, and also digital platforms that distribute content made by marginalised groups in particular. The chapter 3 example of *gal–dem* illustrates how independent media keen to avoid corporate co-optation face often insuperable economic challenges, resulting in their workers – particular those from racially minoritised and working-class backgrounds – receiving the lowest rewards for their labour.

Given this, pluralism of this kind requires forms of public funding for independent media run by marginalised communities. This is particularly important as there has been a rapid decline of media outlets once deemed 'alternative' and a 'gateway' to the industry for racially minoritised and precariously positioned workers (e.g., Bitch Media, gal–dem, i-D, Vice). Independent media, by definition, provide the most autonomy for people structurally positioned by race and class. They allow them to tell stories in the way that they want to tell them, whether about racial injustice or not.

The foundation of this specific proposal is a form of political and economic redress, where national governments acknowledge that racialised groups, whose positioning in 'the West' has either directly or indirectly been the product of empire and colonial excursion, have been historically marginalised and excluded. Reparative justice provides one potential framework for the state to fund independent media for those who belong to communities structurally defined by race and where previous generations were often silenced by colonial power. Public funding of this kind acts as a form of repair, reconstituting the nation in a way that benefits all its communities.

This kind of reconstitution must be accompanied by imaginative reforms of Public Service Media (PSM). These institutions, across different national contexts, are in an embattled state, thanks to attacks from right-wing governments and intense competition from wealthier global media conglomerates. While PSM has historically tended towards supporting elite agendas rather than fully catering to the needs and desires of all the nation's communities, this manifesto contends that it still plays a crucial role in anti-racist media ecosystem and needs to be reinvigorated and supported. An anti-racist PSM depends on three conditions being met. Firstly, to repeat, there need to be more sustained efforts to increase the number of people from under-represented communities at the senior level. This demands not just greater transparency, but making recruitment more *democratic* to halt a situation where the dominant culture and elite political circles are effectively allowed to insert their own members into key roles and positions.

Secondly, governments need to undo decades of neoliberal creep and buffer PSM from commercial pressures. This also demands confronting the funding crisis of PSM and ensuring that they can compete on a level playing field with commercial media. Thirdly, the remit of PSM to cater fully for all the nation's communities, no matter how small, should be made more central to its output. This is the real value of PSM, and in a digital era it can encompass dissemination and amplification, not just representation. On digital platforms, PSM must foreground programmes made by under-represented communities, including the development of anti-racist algorithms that can help audiences find more 'diverse' content in a way that makes pluralism a dimension of everyday media flow.

Thinking about the shift from Public Service Broadcasting (PSB) to PSM aids us in emphasising the importance of pluralist public spaces to an anti-racist media future. This involves questioning the prevalent assumption that digital media are inherently more accessible and inclusive than print alternatives. Digital media clearly play a formative role in contemporary media ecologies, but other media formats remain important and some have important anti-racist potential.

As a *Fortune* article highlights, 'Tech giants have gutted publishing. Now digital fatigue is giving print a new lease on life' (Miller 2023). That is, there is continued demand for print media; findings from YouGov's 2022 poll of more than 111,600 people in the UK suggest that 58% of respondents prefer print magazines to digital (Bansal 2022). Print media has played a crucial part in the legacy of anti-racist organising, for particular reasons. Unlike the creation of digital content, the production of grassroots print media, such as local news publications and movement manifestos, can be *relatively* free from the intervening gaze and powers of tech giants. Acknowledging this does not mean portraying print media and its production as a panacea. Rather, we view an anti-racist media future as being one that requires racially minoritised people to have control of the means of media production, and we see a key opportunity to do so in relation to print.

Towards an Anti-Racist Media

Instead of simply accepting the decline of print media as given, an anti-racist media future must find ways to foster the creation and flourishing of anti-racist printed press. After all, the circulation of print media such as newspapers and newsletters at protests and community gatherings continues to play an important role in mobilising anti-racist movements and actions. As chapter 4 discussed, forms of local and citizen journalism can be central to anti-racist media landscapes. Building these capacities will require the creation and establishment of more media cooperatives that yield both print *and* digital media. Supporting community-owned and collectively created media is critical to combating the dominant flow of shallow and gestural forms of corporate anti-racism. An anti-racist media future is one that supports citizen and local journalism, such as by equipping communities with the resources to build self-sustaining and grassroots infrastructures (e.g., local radio and print publications). It challenges the media industry's preoccupation with pivoting to video and moving away from print, by investing in long-form and long-term journalism that yields media in a wide range of formats – digital and analogue.

Thus, an anti-racist media future must cultivate a sense of collectivism to ensure that the means of media production are accessible to, and can be collectively owned by, racially diverse communities. Accordingly, we believe that an anti-racist media future is one that must be radically accessible in ways that account for the interconnected nature of oppressions.

*　*　*

Our manifesto focuses on the path that may lie ahead, underpinned by an understanding of the history of anti-racist organising and media. While an anti-racist media future is one that ensures that the design, production and circulation of media occurs in accessible ways, it is also a media future that establishes and maintains boundaries. That is, an anti-racist media future requires steadfast commitment to blocking the lucrative circulation of racist discourse, and working to extract media practices and processes from the reproduction of systemic racism.

These ideas and proposals will not automatically lead to *better* representation in media, nor should we place that burden to do so on individual Black, Brown or Asian cultural workers whether they operate in news or popular culture. All media workers and those who engage with media can imagine anti-racist media commitments and practices that, in fact, do not solely work for the benefit of the marginalised. They also increase the pluralism, accuracy, relevance and democratic value of media for the whole of society.

Notes

2 *Out of Balance*

1 A transcript of the documentary can be accessed here: https://www.bcu.ac.uk/media/research/sir-lenny-henry-centre-for-media-diversity/representology-journal /articles/it-aint-half-racist-mum-transcript and it can be viewed here: https://www.youtube.com/watch?v= a-7CqOKD5c8

2 According to Nieman Reports, the proximity of the extreme police violence meted out to Black Lives Matter protests and the successful white nationalist storming of the Capitol six months later led to an insistent posing of the question, *what if the people storming the Capitol had been Black*? They document changing patterns in reporting of police violence, where 'A new coverage dynamic is emerging. Outlets are crowdsourcing video investigations of police use of force, centering accounts from demonstrators and

police violence victims rather than police accounts and concerns about property damage. Newsrooms are taking an interdisciplinary approach to reporting, scrutinising, for example, the relationship between tech corporations and police monitoring activists' social media feeds. And reporters are telling more in-depth stories about victims of police violence, without fixating on the killing or digging into the victim's past to highlight criminality.' See Emmanuel (2021) https://niemanreports.org/articles/spurred-by-black-lives-matter-coverage-of-police-violence-is-changing/

3 Details of the case, see Folkenflik (2020): https://www.npr.org/2020/06/08/872234014/editors-barred-a-black-reporter-from-covering-protests-then-her-news room-rebelled

5 Towards an Anti-Racist Media

1 See the 2022/23 impact report: https://creativeaccess.org.uk/wp-content/uploads/2023/07/Impact-report-2023.pdf

2 https://stopfundinghate.info/ and see https://www.20minutes.fr/high-tech/2133679-20170920-sleeping-giants-comment-toucher-porte-monnaie-sites-fake-news

3 https://www.mediareform.org.uk/

References

Alamo-Pastrana, C., & W. Hoynes (2020) 'Racialization of News: Constructing and Challenging Professional Journalism as "White Media"'. *Humanity & Society* 44(1): 67–91.

Amponsah, E.-L. (2023) 'Black Dis/Engagement: Negotiating Mainstream Media Presence and Refusal'. *European Journal of Cultural Studies* 21(8): 1285–1301.

Anderson, W. C. (2020) 'The Disregard of Power in Journalistic "Objectivity"', Hyperallergic. https://hyperallergic.com/569848/the-disregard-of-power-in-journalistic-objectivity/ (accessed 12 January 2024).

Andrejevic, M. (2013) Infoglut: *How Too Much Information Is Changing the Way We Think and Know*. New York and London: Routledge.

Argeudas, A., S. Banerjee, C. Mont'Alverne, B. Toff, R. Fletcher, R. K. Nielsen (2023) *News for the Powerful and Privileged: How Misrepresentation and Under-Representation of Disadvantaged Communities Undermine Their Trust in News*. Oxford: Reuters Institute.

Bailey, M. (2021) *Misogynoir Transformed: Black Women's Digital Resistance*. New York: New York University Press.

Bailey, M., & Trudy (2018) 'On Misogynoir: Citation, Erasure and Plagiarism'. *Feminist Media Studies* 18(4): 762–768.

Bansal, B. (2022) 'US/GB: Consumers May Prefer Their News Online, but for Magazines It's a Different Matter', YouGov, 27 September. https://business. yougov.com/content/43701-usgb-consumers-may-prefer-their-news-online-magazi.

Barnett, S., & J. Petley (2022) 'Why Ofcom Must Find Its Backbone', *The British Journalism Review* 32(1): 29–36.

BBC News (2014) 'Lenny Henry Criticises BBC Chief's Diversity Plans'. 24 June. http://www.bbc.co.uk/news /entertainment-arts-27992392 (accessed 4 October 2016).

Benkler, Y., R. Faris, H. Roberts (2018) *Network Propaganda: Manipulation, Disinformation and Radicalization in American Politics*. Cambridge: Cambridge University Press.

Birhane, A. (2021) 'Algorithmic Injustice: A Relational Ethics Approach', Patterns 2(2): 100205.

References

Birhane, A. (2022) 'The Unseen Black Faces of AI Algorithms', *Nature* 610: 451–453.

Bremner, F. (2023) 'Reacting to Black Lives Matter: The Discursive Construction of Racism in UK Newspapers'. *Politics* 43(3): 298–314.

Brook, O. et al. (2020) *Culture Is Bad for You*. Manchester: Manchester University Press.

Buccola, N. (2019) *The Fire Is upon Us*. Princeton, NJ: Princeton University Press.

Canella, G. (2023) 'Journalistic Power: Constructing the "Truth" and the Economics of Objectivity'. *Journalism Practice* 17(2): 209–225.

Carrington, D. (2018) 'BBC Admits "We Get Climate Change Coverage Too Wrong Often"', *The Guardian*, 7 September.

Creative Access (2023) *Impact Report*. https://creativeac cess.org.uk/wp-content/uploads/2023/07/Impact-report-2023.pdf (accessed 5 April 2024).

Davis, G. (2024) 'Revealed: The Shocking Tweets of GB News Co-owner Sir Paul Marshall', Hope Not Hate. https://hopenothate.org.uk/2024/02/22/revealed-the -shocking-tweets-of-gb-news-co-owner-sir-paul-marshall/ (accessed 27 February 2024).

Distributed AI Research Institute (DAIR) (n.d.) https:// www.dair-institute.org/ (accessed 5 April 2024).

Emmanuel, A. (2021) 'Spurred by Black Lives Matter, Coverage of Police Violence Is Changing'. Nieman Reports. https://niemanreports.org/articles/spurred-by

References

-black-lives-matter-coverage-of-police-violence-is
-changing/ (accessed 5 April 2024).

Esser, F., & A. Umbricht (2014) 'The Evolution of Objective and Interpretative Journalism in the Western Press'. *Journalism and Mass Communication Quarterly* 91(2): 229–249.

European Race and Imagery Foundation (2023) 'ERIF'. https://erifonline.org (accessed 15 July 2023).

Fenton, N., D. Freedman, J. Schlosberg, L. Dencik (eds) (2020) *The Media Manifesto*. Cambridge: Polity Press.

Folkenflik, D. (2020) 'Editors Barred a Black Reporter from Covering Protests. Then Her Newsroom Rebelled', NPR, 8 June. https://www.npr.org/2020/06/08/872234014/editors-barred-a-black-reporter-from-covering-protests-then-her-newsroom-rebelled (accessed 12 November 2023).

Frazer-Carroll, M. (2020) 'Don't Call Me. . .'. British Journalism Review 31(1): 12–14.

Frenkel S., & K. Conger (2022) 'Hate Speech's Rise on Twitter Is Unprecedented, Researchers Find'. *The New York Times*, 2 December.

Fullerton, S. (2022) 'Influencers Are Whitewashing Syria's Regime, with Help from Sponsors'. https://www.washingtonpost.com/opinions/2022/08/08/travel-influencers-whitewash-syrian-war/ (accessed 15 July 2023).

gal–dem (2023) 'Goodbye from gal–dem'. *gal–dem*,

References

31 March. https://gal-dem.com/gal-dem-goodbye-letter/ (accessed 25 March 2024).

Glitch (2020) 'Covid-19 and the Epidemic of Online Abuse. End Violence against Women'. https://www.endviolenceagainstwomen.org.uk/wp-content/uploads/Glitch-and-EVAW-The-Ripple-Effect-Online-abuse-during-COVID-19-Sept-2020.pdf (accessed 26 March 2024).

Glitch (2023) 'The Digital Misogynoir Report: Ending Dehumanising of Black Women on Social Media'. https://glitchcharity.co.uk/wp-content/uploads/2023/07/Glitch-Misogynoir-Report_Final_18Jul_v5_Single-Pages.pdf (accessed 25 November 2023).

Gray, H. (2016) 'Precarious Diversity: Representation and Demography'. In: Curtin, M. & Sanson, K. (eds) *Precarious Creativity: Global Media, Local Labour*. Oakland, CA: University of California Press.

Hall, S. (1988) 'New Ethnicities'. In: Mercer, K. (ed.) *Black Film British Cinema*. London: Institute of Contemporary Art.

Hampton, R. (2019) 'The Black Feminists Who Saw the Alt-Right Coming'.
https://slate.com/technology/2019/04/black-feminists-alt-right-twitter-gamergate.html (accessed 25 November 2023).

Harry, S. (2021) 'Listening to Black Women: The Innovation Tech Can't Figure Out'. *Wired*, 11 January. https://www.wired.com/story/listening-to-black-

References

women-the-innovation-tech-cant-figure-out/ (accessed 25 November 2023).

Havens, T. (2013) *Black Television Travels: African American Media Around the Globe*. New York: NYU Press.

Hirsch, A. et al. (2019) 'You Can't Be Impartial about Racism – An Open Letter to the BBC on the Naga Munchetty Ruling', *The Guardian*, 27 September.

Høeg, E., & C. D. Tulloch (2019) 'Sinking Strangers: Media Representations of Climate Refugees on the BBC and Al Jazeera'. *Journal of Communication Inquiry* 43(3): 225–248.

Jackson, S. J., M. Bailey, B. Foucault Welles (2020) *#HashtagActivism: Networks of Race and Gender Justice*. Cambridge, MA: MIT Press.

Kundnani, A. (2023) *What Is Antiracism? And Why It Means Anticapitalism*. London: Verso.

Lentin, A. (2019) *Why Race Still Matters*. Cambridge: Polity Press.

Littler, J. (2017) *Against Meritocracy: Culture, Power and Myths of Mobility*. London: Routledge.

Lowery, W. (2020) 'A Reckoning over Objectivity. Led by Black Journalists'. *The New York Times*, 23 June.

McMillan Cottom, T. (2021) 'Where Platform Capitalism and Racial Capitalism Meet: The Sociology of Race and Racism in Digital Society'. *Sociology of Race and Ethnicity* 6(4): 441–449.

References

Menuge, E., L. Peillon, B. Renard (2023) 'CNews, chaîne "pluraliste"? Passage au crible d'une semaine d'invités sur la chaïne d'info', *Libération*, 15 July.

Miller, D. (2023) 'Tech Giants Have Gutted Publishing. Now Digital Fatigue Is Giving Print a New Lease on Life'. *Fortune*, 25 May. https://fortune.com/2023/05/25/tech-giants-have-gutted-publishing-now-digital-fatigue-is-giving-print-a-new-lease-on-life/ (accessed 25 March 2024).

Noble, S. U. (2018) *Algorithms of Oppression: How Search Engines Reinforce Racism*. New York: New York University Press.

Olivares, V. (2019) 'Journalists of Color Urge Newsrooms to Call Out Racism', *Latino Reporter*, 5 September.

Parham, J. (2023) 'Black Twitter Remains Unbothered in Elon Musk's X'. *Wired*, 29 January. https://www.wired.com/story/black-twitter-post-elon-musk-x/ (accessed 25 March 2024).

Pew Research Center (2023) 'Black Americans' Experiences with News'. *Pew Research Center*. https://www.pewresearch.org/journalism/2023/09/26/black-americans-experiences-with-news/ (accessed 25 March 2024).

Reid, J. C., & Craig, M. O. (2021) 'Is It a Rally or a Riot? Racialized Media Framing of 2020 Protests in the United States'. *Journal of Ethnicity in Criminal Justice* 19(3–4): 291–310.

References

Reporters sans Frontières (2024) 'Sur un recours de RSF, la décision historique du Conseil d'État dans le dossier Arcom/CNews'. 13 February. https://rsf.org/fr/france-s ur-un-recours-de-rsf-la-d%C3%A9cision-historique-du-conseil-d-%C3%A9tat-dans-le-dossier-arcomc news (accessed 5 April 2024).

Renton, D. (2019) *The New Authoritarians: Convergence on the Right*. London: Pluto.

Sanson, K. (ed.) *Precarious Creativity*. Oakland, CA: University of California Press.

Sivanandan, A. (1990) *Communities of Resistance: Writing on Black Struggles for Socialism*. London: Verso.

UCLA Entertainment and Media Research Initiative (2023) *Hollywood Diversity Report 2023*. https:// socialsciences.ucla.edu/hollywood-diversity-report -2023/ (accessed 26 March 2024).

Valluvan, S. (2019) *The Clamour of Nationalism*. Manchester: Manchester University Press.

Wallace, L. R. (2019) *The View from Somewhere: Undoing the Myth of Journalistic Objectivity*. Chicago: The University of Chicago Press.

Warner, K. J. (2017) 'In the Time of Plastic Representation'. *Film Quarterly* 71(2). https://film quarterly.org/2017/12/04/in-the-time-of-plastic-representation/ (accessed 5 April 2024).

Williams, A., M. Miceli, T. Gebru (2022) 'The Exploited Labor behind Artificial Intelligence'. https://

References

www.noemamag.com/the-exploited-labor-behind-artificial-intelligence/ (accessed 15 July 2023).

Younge, G. (2021) 'What Covid Taught Us about Racism – And What We Need to Do Now'. *The Guardian*, 16 December. https://www.theguardian.com/society/2021/dec/16/systemic-racism-covid-gary-younge (accessed 25 March 2024).

Zelizer, B., C. W. Anderson, P. J. Boczkowski (2021) *The Journalism Manifesto*. Cambridge: Polity Press.